HUMPTY DUMPTY

and other plays

Books by Eric Bogosian available from TCG

THE ESSENTIAL BOGOSIAN
(*Talk Radio, Drinking in America, Funhouse, Men Inside*)

HUMPTY DUMPTY AND OTHER PLAYS
(Includes *Griller, Red Angel, Non-Profit Benefit*)

NOTES FROM UNDERGROUND
(Also includes *Scenes from the New World*)

POUNDING NAILS IN THE FLOOR WITH MY FOREHEAD

SEX, DRUGS, ROCK & ROLL

subUrbia

WAKE UP AND SMELL THE COFFEE

HUMPTY DUMPTY

and other plays

ERIC BOGOSIAN

THEATRE COMMUNICATIONS GROUP
NEW YORK
2005

Humpty Dumpty and Other Plays is published by Theatre Communications Group, Inc., 520 Eighth Avenue, 24th Floor, New York, NY 10018-4156.

This publication is made possible in part with public funds from the New York State Council on the Arts, a State Agency.

TCG books are exclusively distributed to the book trade by Consortium Book Sales and Distribution, 1045 Westgate Dr., St. Paul, MN 55114.

Library of Congress Cataloging-in-Publication Data

Bogosian, Eric.
Humpty Dumpty and other plays / Eric Bogosian.— 1st ed.
p. cm.
ISBN-13: 978-1-55936-251-1
ISBN-10: 1-55936-251-0
I. Title.
PS3552.O46H86   2005
812'.54—dc22
2005023820

Book design and composition by Lisa Govan
Cover art and design by John H Howard
Author photo by Mark Seliger

First Edition, November 2005

To my beloved teacher, Dottie Welling, who started it all

Contents

Preface

What you have in your hands is the end result of workshops, table reads and productions in Chicago, Baltimore, Princeton, Williamstown and San Jose of my three most recent plays. I have revised each play for this edition.

A playscript is something like an engineer's blueprint for a marvelous machine. No matter how cool it looks on paper, the only way to see if the thing works is to build it and run it. With playwriting, unlike most literature, what you see is *not* what you get. The dialogue on the page indicates a game plan which comes to life only after it has been interpreted by a director and a cast and presented to an audience.

Reading a playscript, even reading it out loud, gives only a vague sense of the play's functionality. A great table read may have everyone in the room rolling with laughter or moved to tears, but that doesn't mean the play will "work" onstage. How do you convey the strengths of a play without fully mounting it? You can't. Drama exists under and between the words. A "read" cannot convey the charisma of the actors onstage or the presence of an expectant audience. I wonder if Beckett's plays would have survived if they had to pass muster through the table-read/workshop system we have in place now.

Because a play must be staged to be fully known, it's almost impossible to disseminate drama to a large audience (large as in "mass media" large) without either recording it on film (which never really succeeds in capturing what makes a live play exciting) or having it published in script form. The plays in this volume were performed all over the United States, but to my dismay, not in New York City where I live. If you weren't there in Chicago or Princeton or San Jose, you missed them. In some cases, they were reviewed after one or two previews, without the benefit of revisions or adjustments. And thus their fate was sealed with gentle praise or harsh criticism by the pundits. Whatever.

I present them here not so much as complete works, rather as blueprints for inspection and possible production. Who knows? They may even get mounted in a theater where my peers in New York (my tribe) can come see them some day.

Which brings me to my next cluster of sour grapes: Every performance of a play is a special event and it lives through its audience as much as through its players. In effect, each audience is co-author of the event. The author of a play cannot create a play in a vacuum (exception—mad geniuses). An audience with a point-of-view needs theater with a point-of-view. Audiences with nothing at stake want plays with nothing at stake. Audiences at risk demand plays about risk. Good theater reflects the priorities of the community. My tribe knows what it wants and being judged by the needs of another group is, as far as I'm concerned, pointless.

In short, I hope you (the reader) find that these plays speak to you, because these plays reflect hard questions churning within me, conjured in the only way I know how to think—through character and dialogue.

Two dozen thank yous, in no particular order: Terry Nemeth, Kathy Sova, Amanda Burroughs Moran, Philip Rinaldi, Jill Rachel Morris, Anne Cattaneo, Robert Falls, André Bishop, Michael Ritchie, George Lane, Fred Zollo, Nick Paleologos, Emily Mann, Mara Isaacs, Janice Paran, Bernie Telsey, Will Cantler, David Vaccari, Daniel Swee, Derek McLane, Charles McNulty, Claudia Cross and, of course, Jo Bonney.

—**E.B.**
New York
October 2005

GRILLER

The scheme for *Griller* took shape when Anne Cattaneo called asking if I could contribute some pages for Lincoln Center Theater's Director's Lab for Rob Urbinati. I said: "Yes," and ended up writing the first draft of a short play.

I had worked with Robert Falls on the ecstatic production of *subUrbia* at Lincoln Center and so it made sense to take it to the next step with him. *Griller* ended up at the Goodman in Chicago. The production was elaborate and wild, featuring a genuine swimming pool onstage. And a magnificent cast.

Wanting to look at the play from a different angle, David Warren and I brought it to CENTERSTAGE in Baltimore. Derek provided another wonderful set, and another gang of wildly talented people brought it to life.

—E.B.

Production History

Griller was first presented by the Director's Lab at Lincoln Center Theater (André Bishop, Artistic Director; Bernard Gersten, Executive Producer) in New York, in the spring of 1996. The director was Rob Urbinati, and Leslie Ayvazian, Lynn Cohen, Jerry Grayson, Adam Lamberg, Nicole Marcks, Tom Mardirosian, Tom McCarthy, Mark Rosenthal and Karen Shallo made up the cast. It was then read at Lincoln Center Theater on September 10, 1998. The director was Daniel Sullivan, and Liam Ahern, Lynn Cohen, David Lansbury, Elizabeth Marvel, Mark Rosenthal, Deborah Rush, John Seitz, Karen Shallo and Tony Ward made up the cast.

Griller received its world premiere in Chicago at The Goodman Theatre (Robert Falls, Artistic Director; Roche Edward Schulfer, Executive Director) on January 9, 1998. It was directed by Robert Falls; the set design was by Derek McLane, the costume design was by Mara Blumenfeld, the lighting design was by Kenneth Posner, the sound design was by Richard Woodbury; the dramaturg was Tom Creamer, the stage manager was T. Paul Lynch and the production stage manager was Joseph Drummond. The cast was as follows:

GUSSIE	Robert Klein
MICHELLE	Karen Valentine

DYLAN	Mark Ruffalo
TERENCE	Marc Grapey
ROZ	Nahanni Johnstone
JEREMY	Alex Kirsch
GLORIA	Caroline Aaron
GRANMA BETTY	Irma St. Paule
UNCLE TONY	Howard Witt

These actors helped shape the play during workshops prior to production: Rengin Altay, Michael Guido, Carol Gutierrez, Steve Key, Stephanie March, Ben Pardo, Paul Ratcliff, Barbara Robertson, Carmen Roman, Mary Seibel and Fred Stone.

Griller received a production in Baltimore at CENTERSTAGE (Irene Lewis, Artistic Director; Peter W. Culman, Managing Director) in November–December 1999. It was directed by David Warren; the set design was by Derek McLane, the costume design was by Susan Hilferty, the lighting design was by Donald Holder; the sound designer and composer was John Gromada, the dramaturg was Jill Rachel Morris and the stage manager was Julianne Franz. The cast was as follows:

GUSSIE	David Garrison
MICHELLE	Caitlin Clarke
DYLAN	Chelsea Altman
TERENCE	Josh Radnor
ROZ	Vera Cox
JEREMY	Drew Ansbacher, Christopher Field
GLORIA	Cheryl Giannini
GRANMA BETTY	Scotty Bloch
NICK	Henry Woronicz

Characters

GUSSIE, the griller, retired, fifty-four
MICHELLE, his wife, forty-eight
DYLAN, Gussie and Michelle's son, twenty-eight
TERENCE, Gussie and Michelle's son, thirty-two
ROZ, Terence's wife, thirty-two
JEREMY, Roz and Terence's son, six
GLORIA, Gussie's sister, forty-eight
GRANMA BETTY, Gussie and Gloria's mother, seventy-eight
UNCLE TONY, a friend of the family, mid-seventies

Setting

Gussie's backyard in suburban New Jersey, Fourth of July.

ACT ONE

In black, the staccato bongo and maraca beat of "Sympathy for the Devil" fades up. As we hear: "Please allow me to introduce myself..." a voice can be heard singing along.

Lights up on a suburban house and backyard. Gussie, fifty-four, singing with the music as he prepares his barbecue: sorting his vegetables, his cooking implements, his sauces. Gussie is a self-made man. His white-gray hair is longish, perhaps tied in a short ponytail. Half-glasses hang on a string around his neck, and his baggy shorts and Teva sandals belie a certain hipness. He almost knows every word to the song:

GUSSIE: "... who killed the Kennedys? Well after all, it was you and me ..."

> *(Uncle Tony, mid-seventies, big and fit, emerges from the house in a Hawaiian shirt, with a bottle of beer. He wanders past the griller, finds a chair and plops into it. He flips through the papers.*

Roz, thirty-two, a hardbody in a bikini, enters dripping wet from the pool. She towels off and slathers herself with sunblock.

Jeremy, six, also in a bathing suit, runs out of the house and up to the griller. He touches it.)

DON'T TOUCH THAT Jeremy! It could be hot.

JEREMY: It's not hot Grampa.

(Gussie snaps off the music with a remote control. Roz, noticing the music has stopped, picks up a portable CD player and begins listening. She reclines on a yard chair. She continues slathering.)

GUSSIE: It could be. It could be. Just stay away from it. OK, little guy? Roz?

(Roz can't hear him. Tony puts down the paper to watch Gussie.)

OK. OK, so watch this Jeremy. Grampa's going to show you how to make a *fire*.

(Gussie lifts the lid of the massive barbecue.)

See, you don't need coals because those are "magic rocks" from inside a real volcano . . .

TONY: So, how much that thing cost you?

GUSSIE: Not that much, guy gave me a deal.

TONY: What kind of "deal"?

GUSSIE: Did this whole routine so it gets shipped in from out of state—yada, yada—no tax . . . *(To Jeremy)* So all Grampa has to do is push this button . . .

JEREMY: Can *I* push it?

GUSSIE: Just let Grampa push it for now. See how it turns red? That means it's *hot*.

JEREMY: What does *this* button do?

GUSSIE: That's if Grampa wants to talk to Granma in the house. It's called an "intercom."

ROZ: Jeremy, do you have sunblock on? Come here, let me see you.

(Jeremy goes to his mother, who covers him with sunblock as she continues to listen to her music.)

TONY: Hey "Grampa," how much?

GUSSIE: Five grand and change. No tax.

TONY: You're shitting me.

GUSSIE *(Ignoring Tony)*: Jeremy, see this? This is for ice! See the ice cubes in there?

TONY: You can go around the world for five grand. You can go first class to Vegas and have enough left over for chips and hookers.

GUSSIE: If I want "chips and hookers," Tony, I'll get chips and hookers. I want to *kick back*. Why should I be stuck in a smoky casino when I can be in my beautiful backyard cooking? I grill, I relax. I get mellow. It's like therapy.

(Jeremy, fully sunblocked, grabs a pair of tongs and starts pulling bits of grass out of the ground.)

Jeremy, give me those. Don't do that. Now c'mon, help Grampa! Roz?

(Roz is oblivious, flipping through a magazine with her headphones on.)

MICHELLE *(Off)*: GUS? YOU WANT SOME CRACKERS WITH TAPENADE?

GUSSIE *(Into the intercom)*: Use the intercom!

MICHELLE *(Off)*: WHAT?

GUSSIE *(Shouts to her)*: USE THE INTERCOM!

MICHELLE *(Off)*: What are you talking about?

(Gussie steps closer to the house.)

GUSSIE *(Shouts)*: THE INTERCOM I SHOWED YOU THIS MORN-
ING! IT'S ON THE WALL! NEXT TO THE PHONE!

(Silence. Gussie moves to Roz, who is still blithely unaware.)

(To Roz) You want tapenade?
ROZ: What?
GUSSIE: TAPENADE?

(Roz takes off her headphones.)

ROZ: Jeremy, what are you doing?
JEREMY: Mommy, can I have a beer?
ROZ: Maybe later. If you're real quiet and stay in that chair for at
least five minutes with no talking.

(Jeremy sulks into a chair as Gussie moves toward the house.)

GUSSIE: NO TAPENADE!
TONY: I bought a barbecue at Woolworth's in 1958. I still have it.
Cost me ten bucks.
GUSSIE: You cannot compare a ten-dollar barbecue with this.
TONY: Why not?

(Roz, sans earphones, wanders over to the griller.)

ROZ: Gussie this is *so* cool.
GUSSIE: Yeah. Stand back, it's cool but it's hot.
ROZ: Michelle said you can bake bread in it. Let's bake some bread.
What does *this* do?
GUSSIE: Don't touch that! Don't! Listen, don't touch anything!
You're going to ruin the whole configuration.
ROZ: Gus, you're not flying Apollo 13 here. Just tell me what it does!
GUSSIE: That's if I want to *broast* or if I want to *broil*. Like that. OK?
ROZ: Let's "broast." We could broast some radicchio! Have you ever

done that? Or whole garlic cloves! Or asparagus—have you ever grilled asparagus?

GUSSIE: Look, the menu's set. No broasting today.

MICHELLE *(Off)*: Roz?

ROZ: Yeah? *(To Jeremy)* Stay!

(Roz goes into the house. Gussie squints as he gets a bit of smoke in his eyes.)

GUSSIE: Wow. How nice is this? I'm standing in the middle of my perfect backyard under the beautiful old maples with this amazing . . . appliance, this technical work of art, grilling *meat* . . . like my father did and his father before him, all the way back into ancient history. Father to son. Generation to generation. My children are coming to visit me for my birthday. We have food, we have peace, we have love. It's spiritual. *(Into the intercom)* Michelle, bring your old man a glass of wine when you come out.

MICHELLE *(Off)*: ARE YOU TALKING TO ME?

(Jeremy is out of his chair and under the griller.)

GUSSIE *(Noticing Jeremy)*: Jeremy don't touch that, you're gonna burn your hands now.

JEREMY: What are these Grampa?

GUSSIE: Those are wheels, if you want to roll it somewhere.

TONY: For five grand you should be able to drive the damn thing. I bought a Ford Falcon in 1967 cost less than that.

GUSSIE: And in '67, I was a college dropout bopping to The Kinks. That was then, this is now. You don't like it, order pizza.

JEREMY: Yeah! Let's have pizza instead of barbecue!

GUSSIE: Jeremy, honey, why don't you go swim for a while?

JEREMY: I just got dried off!

GUSSIE: Go ahead. I'll call if I need you.

(Jeremy exits.)

JEREMY *(Off)*: Grampa, look! *(Splash)*

(Roz returns with a bowl of Doritos, some clam dip, goat cheese, etc., and places it all on a table. She sees Jeremy in the pool.)

ROZ: Jeremy! What are you doing in the pool! I just did your sunblock!

JEREMY *(Off)*: Grampa doesn't want to play with me.

ROZ: Grampa's busy right now. Here. Eat something.

(Roz bends over to offer Jeremy some Doritos. Tony checks out her butt.)

TONY: You remind me of someone I knew in Thailand. Gus, did I ever tell you what Toi-Mai could do with a Ping-Pong ball? Amazing coordination.

JEREMY: I play Ping-Pong with Daddy!

GUSSIE: Speaking of Daddy, where is he? It's four o'clock, Roz! I'm cooking already.

ROZ: Where do you think he is? At the office. Then he has to pick up Dylan.

GUSSIE *(Putting whole peppers and onions on the griller)*: These are beauties . . .

ROZ *(To Tony)*: Were you in *Phuket*? I hear Phuket is amazingly cool.

TONY: No. Other end. North. Chang Mai. Near Burma.

GUSSIE: Tony doesn't like "cool" places, Roz, only the hot ones. The closer to hell the better.

TONY: Hell is cool. Hell is very cool.

ROZ: I'd love to hang out in Thailand, or you know, *Tibet*. Gussie only gets us tickets to Aruba.

GUSSIE: Hey. You guys weren't complaining when I sent you to Nevis last year *free of charge*. *(To Tony)* They got a great deal here, not only does Grampa cover the whole itinerary—food, hotel, rental car—I throw in babysitting on top.

ROZ: We went down to the Caribbean all the time when I was modeling. Every beach has the same blue water, same stupid sand, same boring sunshine.

GUSSIE: Roz, you want to go to Thailand? I'll send you to Thailand. Throw in the chopsticks for free. *(Yells to Michelle)* I'M READY OUT HERE, THIS IS AT PEAK.

(Jeremy enters from the pool. He munches on Doritos.)

JEREMY: Our new house has an even bigger pool than yours, Grampa.

GUSSIE: Not that much bigger.

JEREMY: Mommy hates the neighbors.

ROZ: I don't hate the neighbors. It's just when we bought our place the leaves were on the trees, then in the winter, the leaves fell *off* and we could see their ugly house. It ruins the feeling.

(Michelle, forty-eight, enters carrying a platter of meat. She is wearing the latest ultra-cool sports outfit by Versace. Her hair is dyed and cut in the most expensive, SoHo-chic style.)

MICHELLE: Here you go, O Grand Master of the Patio, the sacrifice for your altar.

(Gussie focuses on Michelle's plate of meat.)

GUSSIE: That's it?

MICHELLE: You've got half the cow there, Gus. If it isn't enough, I'll go get more.

GUSSIE: No! Everyone's going to be here in a few minutes.

JEREMY: I don't want this yucky stuff. Where's the hot dogs?

GUSSIE: He wants hot dogs. *(To Jeremy)* Do you know what's in hot dogs, Jeremy? *Lots* of yucky stuff. Lips. Tongues. Fingers from guys who work on the assembly line. Besides, that meat there cost $18.50 a *pound*, pal.

ROZ: Gus, you know I don't eat meat, right?

GUSSIE: Aww, come on!

MICHELLE: Oh, I've been thinking about doing that. So, you eat fish?

ROZ: Oh yeah. Tons.

MICHELLE: I have some salmon in the freezer.

GUSSIE: No. No salmon! I'm not mixing fish with beef. The fish molecules, they—they fly into the air, float around, next thing you know, they're on the steaks.

(Tony stands up, heads for the house.)

MICHELLE *(Motioning to the cooler):* There's more beer here, Tony.

TONY: That's OK. I need a real drink. I got it.

(Tony exits into the house. Michelle watches him go.)

MICHELLE: He's going for the vodka, Gus.

GUSSIE: Hey Michelle, he's a teddy bear.

MICHELLE: Yeah well the last time "Teddy" was here, he burned a hole in my best rug and spilled Kahlua all over my auto-graphed Hockney catalog.

ROZ: What is he, in the army or something?

GUSSIE: Was. Navy SEAL. Last twenty years he's been working as some kind of a consultant.

ROZ: He's sexy in a weird way. Goes to all those exciting places.

GUSSIE: He's a lone wolf. We never know when he's gonna show up.

ROZ: You think he's killed people?

GUSSIE: In Korea, probably. But now he's just an old guy with too much time on his hands—

MICHELLE *(Sipping her wine):* Who drinks too much.

GUSSIE: This is perfect-o. Yes! *(To Michelle)* Now, I just push this and the dial tells me the exact temperature at the point of contact.

MICHELLE *(To Gussie):* So, is it working?

(Gussie squints at the dial.)

GUSSIE: Why do they make these numbers so small?

MICHELLE: Use your glasses.

GUSSIE *(Defensive)*: I don't need my glasses. It's hot. It's hot. It's fine.

ROZ: Michelle, you have any tofu lying around? I should have some protein.

GLORIA *(Off, singsong)*: HELLOOO!!!???

GUSSIE: WE'RE BACK HERE!

(Michelle exits into the house.

Gloria, Gussie's "little sister," forty-eight, carrying a huge Tupperware bowl of macaroni salad and a wrapped present, enters assisting Granma Betty, seventy-eight, who walks with a large aluminum cane.)

GLORIA: Hold on to me.

GRANMA BETTY: I'm fine! Leggo!

GLORIA: You almost fell down the front steps.

GRANMA BETTY: I wasn't falling.

GLORIA: You didn't fall because I caught you. Strained my back.

GRANMA BETTY: I'm all right, I'm *all right*. Let me go!

(Granma Betty is steered toward a sling chair as Gloria comes over to kiss Gussie. She puts the bowl on the table and immediately goes for the chips.)

GLORIA: Macaroni salad. I made it last night, but I left it out and it got warm. I hope it's all right.

GRANMA BETTY *(To Roz)*: Where are your clothes? You're naked.

(Granma Betty eyes the scary-looking sling chair.)

What's this? A chair? I can't sit in this. Wait a minute.

GLORIA: Just sit down, Ma!

GUSSIE: Ma, relax. Take it easy. Everybody chill. Gloria, have some chips.

GRANMA BETTY: "Take it easy." People take it *too* easy. That's how they get fat. Well, happy birthday, Gus. Now you're old like me.

(Jeremy runs to the pool with a baster. He returns squirting Granma Betty with water.)

GUSSIE: I can still beat you in the hundred-yard dash, Ma. And who says I'm fat? Gloria, am I fat?

GLORIA: Don't listen to her. This is for you. *(Indicating the present)* Happy Birthday. *(To Jeremy)* Jeremy, come here, honey, come see Great Aunt Gloria.

(Jeremy ignores Gloria. Instead he dive-bombs into Granma Betty's lap.)

JEREMY: GREAT Granma Betty!!!

(Gussie unwraps his present. It turns out to be a huge novelty pepper mill in the shape of a garden gnome.)

GUSSIE *(Revealing the gift)*: Awwww! Thanks, Sis. What I always wanted. A *vibrator*!

GRANMA BETTY *(As Jeremy jumps all over her)*: Owww . . . If I hadn't reminded her, she wouldn't have got you anything.

GLORIA: It's not a— *(Forced to say it)* vibrator. It's a *pepper grinder*! Look, you turn his head.

GUSSIE *(Turning the head)*: Ohhh!!! I needed this. Seriously.

GLORIA: They had them on sale at T.J. Maxx. I couldn't resist.

GRANMA BETTY *(To Roz)*: Where's your husband? Gussie, where's Terence?

GUSSIE: He's picking up Dylan in the city.

GRANMA BETTY: What city? *(Jeremy squirms)* Oooofff! Dylan lives in the city?

ROZ: Jeremy. Down. Get down! *Now!*

GUSSIE: He's doing his starving artist thing, Ma. You know. He "needs his space."

JEREMY: Great-Granma Betty, how old are you?

ROZ: Granma Betty's young, Jeremy.

JEREMY: No, she's not. She's gonna be *dead* pretty soon. That's what Daddy said.

ROZ: Wow, Jeremy!!! That's not very nice!

GUSSIE: We're all gonna be dead pretty soon, Jeremy. All depends on how you define "pretty soon."

(Jeremy continues to wrangle with Granma Betty.)

(Indicating the griller) No one has commented on my new acquisition.

(Gloria comes over to inspect the griller.)

GLORIA: It's very impressive, Gus. How much was it?

(Roz, exasperated, grabs Jeremy and plunks him onto the grass. Michelle enters wiping her hands.)

GUSSIE: Oh, not much. See Michelle got me this Rolex. But you know, I had a watch already, and anyway, so what I did—

MICHELLE: He actually *returned* the watch, *bought* the griller and gave me the *change.*

GUSSIE: I *loved* the watch but I prefer—and you knew I was going to do this Michelle so don't say you didn't—to go out and buy myself my own present. Makes life much simpler.

MICHELLE *(Ironic)*: Well, isn't that sweet? The simple life. Next year I'll get you a sundial. *(Changes subject)* So, doesn't everyone look terrific! What a nice blouse, Gloria!

GLORIA: You gave it to me last Christmas.

MICHELLE: It looks different. Did you lose some weight? Hi, Betty. *(Kisses Granma Betty)* So how was traffic?

GLORIA: Ucch. You'd think they were giving stuff away. Everything just stops.

GRANMA BETTY: Because we left *too late*. *(To Michelle)* I tell her, give yourself enough time. She never gives herself enough time. Fussing with her hair! *(To Gloria)* No one's looking at you!

MICHELLE: Gloria, you want anything to drink?

GLORIA: Diet Coke.

(Michelle gets Gloria a soda from the cooler.)

JEREMY: I'm hungry. Grampa, hurry up with the food!

ROZ: Jeremy, we're going to eat when Daddy and Uncle Dylan get here. Go run around or something.

GUSSIE: Jeremy! Be careful of that new grass seed I put down by the path there. *(To Gloria)* You should've taken the bridge. I tell you every time you come here, take the bridge. But you don't listen.

GLORIA: It's those people working on the tunnel, they move like molasses.

MICHELLE: What people?

GLORIA: You can see when you're driving by. They're not working. They're goofing off, drinking coffee. What ever happened to the work ethic?

MICHELLE: Maybe it was their break?

GLORIA: No. You see it all the time. When you're in line in the store, in a diner, everywhere. They're not American, so what do they care?

GUSSIE: Who's not American? Who are you talking about, Gloria?

GLORIA: Oh sure, or they're "minorities." With all their "problems." Like that gardener you've got. And your cleaning lady.

MICHELLE: The gardener is from Nicaragua. He's not a minority. I mean he is, but not from where he's from.

(Michelle goes in the house.)

GLORIA: That's what I'm saying. They're taking our jobs!

GUSSIE: You want to cut my lawn, Gloria? I'm paying ten bucks an hour.

GLORIA: No, I don't want to cut your lawn, Gus! I'm just saying, when was the last time a real American waited on you anywhere? In a store? In a bank? A *real* American. Think. No. It's always these "other" people now. They don't smile. They treat you like dirt. What am I, dirt? And they never say "thank you."

GUSSIE: They have a different value system, Gloria. It's the way they're brought up. It's cultural.

GLORIA: Listen to you, Mr. Bleeding Heart. They're so angry. Why are they angry at *me*? I never did anything to them.

GUSSIE: A lot of them don't have the education. That's what I'm saying. You have to be patient.

GLORIA: Oh, Gus, you always take their side against me.

GRANMA BETTY *(To Gussie)*: Can *I* have something to drink?

GLORIA: It's so easy for you to have this high-and-mighty attitude, with your Rolex watches and your swimming pools and your three-car garage. You're above it all.

GUSSIE: Jesus, Gloria. Sure, Ma, sure, what d'you want?

GRANMA BETTY: Do you have any red wine? Sweet?

GUSSIE: Michelle! DO YOU HAVE ANY SWEET RED WINE FOR MY MOTHER?

MICHELLE *(Over the intercom)*: Use the intercom!

GUSSIE *(Into the intercom)*: A pint of THUNDERBIRD for my mother, please?

GLORIA *(To herself)*: No one's listening to me. I don't know why I bother talking.

GRANMA BETTY: Where's Terence? Did he work today?

GLORIA: Gussie told you, he's in the *city* with Dylan!

GRANMA BETTY: What city?

GLORIA: He's at *work*, Ma! For God's sake. *(To Gussie)* She pretends to be senile, so we don't notice that she really is.

GRANMA BETTY: It's Sunday. Who works on a Sunday?

GUSSIE: Terence works every day, Ma. That's the business he's in. It's Sunday here, but it's Monday morning someplace else.

(Michelle enters with the wine for Granma Betty.)

ROZ: He's a workaholic, Granma Betty. You know what that means? It means if he isn't working, he doesn't know what to do with himself. His idea of fun is more stress. His idea of a vacation is climbing ice-covered rocks with his bare hands. Wish he'd save some of that energy for the bedroom.

GUSSIE: Better a workaholic than an alcoholic.

MICHELLE: Here you go, Betty.

GRANMA BETTY: Lovely.

GUSSIE: OK, I brush this on, seal in the flavor. Stage one completed. Put those aside. —I should have my own TV show: *Grilling with Gus.*

ROZ: No! *The Gourmet Travel Agent.*

GLORIA: No, no! *The Traveling Gourmet!*

(Gloria rummages on the table for more food. Jeremy runs back to the pool.)

GUSSIE: Look at this weather! You couldn't buy this weather. Reminds me of Loveland, Colorado. Huge skies. Crystal blue. Of course I was stoned most of the time I was out there. That might have had something to do with it. *(Laughs to himself)* There was this one time, I was hitching outside of Boulder and I'd just dropped a hit of windowpane—

GLORIA *(Indicating Granma Betty)*: Gus!

GUSSIE: What?! Hey, Ma, you know what windowpane is?

GRANMA BETTY: Of course I know what a windowpane is! What kind of question is that?

GLORIA: He's talking about *drugs*, Ma.

GUSSIE: No, I'm not, actually I'm talking about the weather.

GRANMA BETTY: Did you remember to bring my medicine, Gloria?

GLORIA: Why do I have to remember? Why don't you remember?

GUSSIE: The sky was so blue that day . . . like burning ice.

GRANMA BETTY: See? You don't care about me.

GLORIA: I brought it. I brought it. But you have to take it with your meal.

GRANMA BETTY *(To Gussie)*: She doesn't care.

(Uncle Tony finally reenters, holding a bottle of Johnny Walker in one hand, a bottle of Absolut in the other.)

TONY: I like your bathroom, Gus. A person could set up camp in there.

GUSSIE: Bigger than our first apartment.

TONY: Very relaxing.

GUSSIE: Good. I'm glad. I see you found the booze.

(Tony puts a glass on the table and pours himself three fingers.)

TONY: Hello Betty. How's your blood pressure?

GRANMA BETTY: Never mind about my blood. At least I have blood.

TONY *(To Gloria)*: Hiya, beautiful.

GLORIA: Tony.

(Tony takes his drink and sits near Roz. Jeremy returns from the pool.)

TONY: Nothing like a nice, easy dump. Something to be thankful for. The Hindus say that the sphincter is the mirror of the mind.

GLORIA: Weren't you in China or Japan or something?

TONY: Can't say. If I did, I'd have to kill all of you. *(Laughs)*

GRANMA BETTY: Gussie told me you got lost in the jungle. Got eaten by cannibals.

GUSSIE *(Simultaneously, with Tony)*: I never said that.

TONY *(Simultaneously, with Gussie)*: They tried, they tried. Believe me. I'm not that easy. *(Laughs, looks at Roz)*

JEREMY: What's a "dump"? What's a "spinkter"?

GUSSIE: Never mind, Jeremy.

TONY: A dump is what comes out the other end after you've eaten all that meat your *grampa* is cooking.

JEREMY: "Poop"?

TONY: What a bright kid! Poop—that's right! See, when you get old like Uncle Tony, taking a big dump is all you have to look forward to. Right, Gus?

GUSSIE: I wouldn't know, I'm not old like Uncle Tony. In fact, I had a checkup last week, doctor said I have the blood pressure of a thirty year old. The heartbeat of a twenty year old.

MICHELLE: And the brain of a five year old.

(Gloria laughs.)

GUSSIE: Ha-ha. Very funny, Michelle. You should have your own sitcom.

TONY: Did he stick the digit up the old Hershey Highway? Gotta keep the prostate happy. Unhappy prostate, unhappy man.

GUSSIE: What's that, another Hindu proverb, Tony? I'm very happy. Never been happier.

TONY: Good, because when they cut that sucker out, you're in Pampers for life, and the word "hard" leaves your vocabulary.

GUSSIE: The plumbing is running very smoothly. Right, Michelle?

MICHELLE: Sure, baby. Whatever you say. Has everyone tried the clam dip? It's organic, I got it at Whole Foods.

TONY: I wake up hard, I go to bed hard. Like a rock, like a diamond drill bit. *(Winks at Roz)*

GUSSIE: If we need any drilling, we'll let you know.

TONY: Shark cartilage.

GLORIA: This dip is delicious, Michelle.

TONY: They put me on a diet of shark cartilage. Shrinks the tissue, the prostate.

GUSSIE *(Concentrating on the griller)***:** Oh . . . damn! *(Picks a piece of mushroom off the coals, burns his finger)* Owww! *(Shouts)*

Michelle, you cut these portobellos too small! They're falling through the grill!

(Roz comes over and checks out the meat, aware of the effect she's having on Tony.)

TONY: Sharks never get cancer. No matter how old they are.

ROZ: Oh, a piece dropped through the grill. See? There!

GUSSIE: Can everyone leave me alone to do my job in peace!! Please? For two minutes?

ROZ: Uh, sure. Whatever.

GRANMA BETTY: I have to go to the bathroom.

GLORIA: You want help, Ma?

GRANMA BETTY: No. No. Get away from me.

(Gloria helps Granma Betty up anyway; getting her up the steps and into the house is arduous.)

ROZ: Michelle, is that a deer?

JEREMY: A deer? Where?

MICHELLE: They're all over the place. Ate half the impatiens I put in.

TONY: Call me the next time you see one. I'll take care of it.

ROZ: No!!!

TONY: Venison's a dark meat. You fill the intestines with the boiled blood, make Prussian sausage.

MICHELLE: Yummy.

(Roz exits into the house as Gloria comes back out. She slumps into her seat, grabbing a handful of food.)

GLORIA: She's like a baby! It isn't enough I clean the house once a week, now she wants me to change the curtains and polish her silver. *(Beat)* We got the tests back, Gus.

GUSSIE: Sometimes you have to change the curtains. She's old.

GLORIA: You want me to give you the reports? You can read them yourself.

GUSSIE: Gloria, this is not the time to be talking about tests and reports. It's my birthday party.

GLORIA: Well, when do you want to talk about them?

GUSSIE: Some other time.

GLORIA: Gus.

GUSSIE: Gloria.

MICHELLE: It's getting late. Jeremy, where do you think your daddy is?

JEREMY: Well, maybe a huge gasoline truck stopped across the road and he smashed into it and the gas blew up in a giant fireball and all his skin was burnt off.

(A car horn from offstage.)

DADDY!

(Jeremy leaps up and runs off.)

GLORIA: He's so imaginative.

GUSSIE: Ten more minutes we'd be eating charcoal.

MICHELLE: Gus, relax. They're here.

TONY: The Prussians would hunt deer with dogs. Alsatians. Purebred. They'd fight a bear. In a pack, bite their eyes out. Blind 'em. Tear the flesh off while the thing is still standing. The SS had Alsatians, too.

(Terence, thirty-two, enters, dressed in a Lacoste tennis shirt and chinos, with Jeremy hanging off his leg. Next to him is his brother, Dylan, twenty-eight, in a white T-shirt, jeans and motorcycle jacket. They are arguing.)

GLORIA: Oh, look who's here!

DYLAN: Don't call me ridiculous—

TERENCE: I didn't call you ridiculous. I said the way you *look* at it is ridiculous . . . We're here, forget it.

MICHELLE: Terence, you made it! I was worried.

DYLAN: Oh yeah, "forget it." You beat the guy half to death.

(Through this, Granma Betty enters and hobbles to her seat.)

TERENCE: Don't exaggerate, OK? For the audience. *(To the family)* He's doing this for you guys.

DYLAN: I'm not "doing" anything. *(To Terence)* The guy's nose was *bleeding.*

TERENCE: He wasn't bleeding.

GUSSIE: Who's bleeding?

DYLAN: Hi, Gus. *(Thrusts a package at him)* Happy birthday.

GLORIA: Now what happened?

(Terence pushes Jeremy down. Jeremy starts jumping up and down. Dylan lights a cigarette and sulks in a corner.)

JEREMY: Daddy, Daddy, Daddy, Daddy!

GRANMA BETTY: Wait a minute. I can't hear what they're saying. Terence, did you work today?

TERENCE: Hey, Granma Betty! Yeah, I worked.

GLORIA *(To Terence)*: Don't you say hello to your aunt?

GUSSIE: Someone got hit?

TERENCE *(Kissing his aunt)*: Hey, Aunt Gloria.

GUSSIE: Who was bleeding?

TERENCE: No one got hit.

DYLAN: Liar.

TERENCE: I mean, I just kind of shoved him. I didn't really hit him.

DYLAN: What difference does it make what you call it? You're strong enough to kill him with your bare hands.

MICHELLE: Terence, we were worried.

TERENCE: We're in line at the tunnel, guy comes up to the car—

DYLAN: This poor, defenseless, homeless beggar—

TERENCE: You want to tell it?

DYLAN: You going to tell the truth?

TERENCE: He's washing the windshield with this filthy rag. I wave to him: "Go away," right?

GLORIA: Was the guy white?

GUSSIE: Yo, Terence, how much steak you think you'll eat? Turns out we're a little short—

MICHELLE: Yes, Terence, we're listening.

TERENCE: I open my window, to tell him to get lost. Yes, he was white.

DYLAN: And . . . ?

TERENCE: Dylan, you know what? Shut up. *(To everyone)* I roll down my window, the guy *spits* on me.

GLORIA: Oh my God. See? This is what I'm saying.

MICHELLE: Terence, why did you do that?

TERENCE: What?

MICHELLE: Roll down your window?

GUSSIE: Will you let the kid tell his story for God's sake, Michelle!

TERENCE: So I got out of the car and I smacked him.

JEREMY: Daddy, did you kill him?

(Roz enters and gives Terence a kiss, conspicuously in front of Dylan.)

ROZ: Hi, honey. Rough ride?

TERENCE: Tunnel.

GUSSIE: And . . . ?

TERENCE: Nothing. He was lying there on the ground *pretending* to be hurt, so we left.

DYLAN: Big-dick pissing contest.

GRANMA BETTY: Why did he spit on you?

GUSSIE: Dylan, come here, help me with this.

DYLAN: I just got here, Dad. *Jesus!* Let me get something to drink.

GUSSIE: Well, no beer, OK?

DYLAN: Hey, back off.

(Dylan grabs a Coke and pops it open right in front of Gussie.)

The pathetic thing is you would have killed him if you could.

TERENCE: We got the message, Dylan.

MICHELLE: At least no one got hurt.

(Michelle goes into the house. Roz hands Terence a beer. He pops it open.)

ROZ: Did you wish your father a happy birthday, Terence?

TERENCE: Oh, happy birthday, Dad. Your gift will show up in your trading account on Monday.

GUSSIE: Not more Microsoft, because I was actually thinking of selling what I've got. What do you think?

DYLAN: Oh, here we go!

(Roz and Dylan exchange a glance.)

TERENCE: I dunno, Dad. What did you pay for it?

GUSSIE: Well, some of it's warrants, some of it's on margin—

TERENCE: Dad, listen, if you wanna run with the big dogs you gotta pee in the tall grass.

GUSSIE: You got guys working for you, have *them* figure it out. They *do* work for you, don't they?

TERENCE: Call me on Wednesday after the market closes. I'll sort it out.

GUSSIE *(Making peace)*: Roz was telling us about the remodeling. When will they be finished?

TERENCE: We haven't even started the demolition.

GLORIA: New fireplaces?

ROZ: Eight. One in every bedroom. I'm bringing in a Feng Shui master to place each hearth. And we're only using local granite.

TERENCE: We're still working that out.

ROZ: I have to have a fireplace in my bedroom. It's an essential.

TERENCE: Yeah, for Benjamin Franklin in 1840!

GLORIA: But, Terence, a fireplace at the foot of your bed. That's very romantic.

DYLAN: Franklin wasn't alive in 1840.

TERENCE *(Irritated)*: What, Dylan?

DYLAN *(Sullen)*: Nothing.

ROZ: And a sauna in the master bathroom. There's nothing nicer than staying naked all day.

GLORIA: Ooooooh! I don't think I could do that!

TERENCE: I don't have time to be naked.

GUSSIE: In the old split-level, we had *one* toilet for six people. Now, between this place here, the time-share in Aspen and the beach house, I figure I have fifteen and a half bathrooms.

GRANMA BETTY: You need fifteen bathrooms because you never stop eating.

ROZ: One room will be empty all the time. No furniture. Just a large polished floor with a tatami mat in the middle. And I will go in there and sit. Think about my life. Meditate.

(Dylan wanders off.)

TERENCE: I could buy a used Ferrari for what it cost.

ROZ: So *buy* a used Ferrari, buy a *new* Ferrari, no one's stopping you. Anything would be better than climbing around those stupid rocks.

TERENCE: If I didn't go climbing, Roz, I'd lose my mind.

GUSSIE: It's not dangerous, Roz. I tried it one time.

(Jeremy is hanging on Terence, making a nuisance of himself.)

TERENCE: Of course it's dangerous. But I get up there, I'm hanging over a three-thousand-foot wall of granite, my muscles are burning, the windchill is ten below zero and I'm *good*. I'm very good, because I don't have to think about stock margins or fireplaces or my wife or my kid. All I have to do is stay alive.

GRANMA BETTY: Wait a minute. Terence, did you work today?

TERENCE: Every day, Granma Betty, every day.

GUSSIE: He works every day, Ma.

(Michelle enters with more munchies, a crooked smile on her face.)

TERENCE: I work every day, 'cause the bastards are out there every day. You make one false move, you're dead meat. They're just waiting for it. Like buzzards. Like wild dogs. Hyenas.

GUSSIE: It's the same thing in the travel business.

TERENCE *(Eating chips; somber)***:** No, Dad. It's not.

MICHELLE: You sound tense, Terence.

TERENCE: Of course I'm tense.

GUSSIE: When I road-managed the bands, I *never* slept. Get a phone call two in the morning: "Aerosmith just wrecked a hotel room in Fort Wayne, get your ass down there."

ROZ: Gussie, you knew Aerosmith?

GUSSIE: Oh, yeah. Finally, I said to myself, If I'm gonna kill myself like this, I want to be the one who makes the money. So I started the travel agency. So now I'm dealing with bus operators in the Yucatan. *(Mexican accent)* "I'm sorry, *señor*, the bus is not available. It fell off the cleef." It's all the same Terence, believe me.

TERENCE: Dad—

GLORIA: Jeremy, come to Auntie Gloria.

(Jeremy ignores her. Granma Betty has fallen asleep.)

TERENCE: I'm dying. I'm screaming, "Help!" and it's like I said, "Please pass the salt."

MICHELLE: Terence, have something to eat.

GUSSIE: Same with me. Same with me. Only worse.

TERENCE: *Dad*, I lent this guy some shares out of my account. Worth about fifteen mil. Now he says they're *his* and he's *suing* me on top of it. Every day I go through this.

GLORIA: Fifteen million? *Dollars?*

(Terence cracks his second beer.)

TERENCE: You know what that nice, liberal, touchy-feely school of Jeremy's is gonna cost me next year?

GLORIA: I hate to think.

TERENCE: You don't want to know. More than you make in nine months. And if we don't send him there, what's gonna happen in the year 2010 when the shit really starts to fly?

TONY *(Sleepy)*: Buy him a .9-millimeter and teach him how to shoot it.

GLORIA: But he's so talented! Jeremy, do Grampa's ad.

TERENCE: Aunt Gloria . . .

GLORIA: Come on, honey, stand up on the table.

(Roz proudly watches him as he gets ready for his routine.)

GUSSIE: Do we have to do this right now?

(Jeremy gets on the table, begins the rehearsed routine:)

JEREMY *(Emphatic)*: "Some kids get a bike for their birthday. You know what I got? A trip to Martinique! And you know why? Because my Grampa Gus is Metro's largest operator of vacation tours and adventure packages. Hey, Gus!"

GUSSIE: "What Jeremy?"

JEREMY: "Next year can I go to the *Congo*???"

(Gloria claps. Jeremy bows. Dylan emerges from the house, finds a spot and lights a cigarette.)

ROZ: A makeup guy I used to do fashion shoots with was a big wheel on *Buffy*, so we're gonna get an audition when we go out to Los Angeles.

GLORIA: That's so exciting!

ROZ: Jeremy's agent says he needs a new headshot. Six hundred bucks. The last one didn't show his sex appeal.

GLORIA: It's worth it. You have to invest in the future.

ROZ: I should lighten his hair a bit more. He's still too, you know, "ethnic."

JEREMY *(Still on top of the table)*: Daddy! Mommy! I saw the deer!

ROZ: That's good. You wanna watch some TV before we sit down to eat?

JEREMY: Yeah. Cartoons.

TERENCE: Put something good on.

JEREMY: Wrestling!

(Jeremy runs off.)

GLORIA: Mark my words, that kid's going to be a big star. I just hope he still speaks to me when he makes it.

(Terence's cell phone chimes. He pulls it out of his pocket and starts talking. He searches for privacy.)

TERENCE: Yeah? Hey.

GUSSIE: Celebrity is a mixed blessing. You get all that attention but no privacy.

MICHELLE: Ah, the expert on celebrity!

GUSSIE: I am something of an expert because I have some knowledge of that situation. People know me from the commercials. *(Beat)* I'm not saying I'm a *star*, Michelle.

MICHELLE *(A little drunk)*: You're *my* little star, honey bunny.

GUSSIE *(Miffed)*: That's not the point, Michelle! Look, I've had friends who are stars.

MICHELLE *(Silly)*: What friends?

GLORIA: Gussie, you booked that tour to Iceland for Regis Philbin that time—

GUSSIE: No . . . uh . . . back in the seventies . . . *(Listing)* The guy from Foghat . . . what's his name, and the pedal steel guy in Poco. Flock of Seagulls . . . Steve Tyler.

MICHELLE: *Steve Tyler?* You're telling me Steve Tyler is your *friend?*

GUSSIE: We partied.

(Gussie searches among his ingredients and cooking utensils.)

MICHELLE: Oh, *right.* You partied. You mean you were in the same room at the same time with straws in your noses.

GUSSIE: Michelle, where's the cilantro?

MICHELLE: Oh, they didn't have any.

GUSSIE: Oh. So how am I going to make my special sauce?

MICHELLE: I don't know. Jesus, Gus, use parsley!

GUSSIE: You can't "use parsley." It has to be cilantro—*fresh.* Chopped into the sauce just before I brush it on at the last minute. Otherwise the whole process doesn't work.

MICHELLE: OK.

GUSSIE *(Angrier, almost to himself)*: So we don't have cilantro. We don't have cilantro. OK. *Well,* then we don't have sauce. We don't have sauce—well, so much for my special barbecue.

MICHELLE: Gus.

GUSSIE: Should have gone out to the Sizzler. Less trouble.

MICHELLE *(Placating)*: It's OK, Gus. It'll be fine.

GUSSIE: Could have ordered *pizza!*

MICHELLE: Gus, your steak is wonderful. It will be delicious.

GUSSIE: IT WON'T BE DELICIOUS!

(Silence all around. Granma Betty wakes up.)

GRANMA BETTY: Is it time to eat?

GUSSIE: Yeah, yeah, let's eat. This is done. Are we going in or staying out here?

GLORIA: The flies.

GUSSIE: The corn *is* done, Michelle?

MICHELLE *(Sobered)*: Yes.

(Granma Betty starts hobbling toward the house.
Tony pours himself a drink and watches everyone else. He finally grabs a platter of meat and takes it in. Gussie hands Roz and Gloria platters and bowls of cooked food. They walk toward the house.)

Dylan? Are you joining us?

(Dylan sits smoking. Roz passes closely by him on her way into the house. They exchange glances. Finally Gussie rounds up his stuff and heads inside. Granma Betty is still creeping along toward the house. Terence can be heard on the phone from inside the house.)

TERENCE *(Off)*: Dieter, *Dieter*, don't tell me that. Because that makes no sense at all. He's not going to expose himself like that. He won't. He won't. Well, then *FUCK HIM*. I don't care. There is no agreement. He can sue me. All's fair, Dieter. All's fair.

MICHELLE: Dylan.

DYLAN: Yeah?

MICHELLE: Thanks for coming over. It means a lot to your father.

DYLAN: Sure, Mom.

MICHELLE: Are you OK?

DYLAN: I'm fine. Just a little tired.

MICHELLE: How's the new job?

DYLAN: Sucks. I quit.

MICHELLE: Well, that's news. How are you planning to pay your rent?

DYLAN: It's paid.

(Granma Betty finally makes it into the house.)

MICHELLE: Yes, but Dylan, I can't give you the money every month.

DYLAN: Ma, I'm gonna pay you back!

MICHELLE: OK. You don't have to shout.

DYLAN: I'm still not drinking. That's a big plus.

MICHELLE: Well, that's not the point, is it?

DYLAN: Ma. I can't threaten my sobriety with too much stress.

MICHELLE: Listen, you're not an alcoholic . . . you've just been, I dunno—confused.

DYLAN: I resent that. Here I am, taking every stupid job that comes down the pike, going to those stupid meetings, and you're telling me I'm *not* an alcoholic.

MICHELLE: Well, you're not.

DYLAN: Then why do I have to go those meetings?

MICHELLE: I honestly don't know, Dylan.

DYLAN: You blackmail me into doing something and you don't even know why I'm doing it.

(Michelle hands Dylan a wad of cash.)

MICHELLE: Make sure your father doesn't find out about this. Please.

DYLAN: If I had any guts I'd be a thousand miles from this backyard. Ten thousand miles. Someplace real. You'd never see me again.

MICHELLE: Don't say that.

(Dylan pockets the money and slouches off. Gussie appears in the doorway of the house.)

GUSSIE: What's the story. Is Pablo Picasso joining us for dinner?

MICHELLE: Would you talk to him, please?

GUSSIE: About what?

(Michelle gives Gussie a curt, forced smile and goes in the house. Gussie saunters over to Dylan.)

Hey man, I appreciate your coming by.

DYLAN: It's your birthday. I'm your son. I figured, "What the hell."

GUSSIE: Thanks for the books. *Thus Spake Zarathustra* and *Death of a Salesman*. Is there some kind of connection?

DYLAN: Whatever.

GUSSIE: Dylan, I know you won't believe me, but we all go through it. When I was your age, I thought the world was coming to an end. The Vietnam War just kept going on and on.

Crooks in the government. Ecological disaster around the corner. But you know what? It all worked out.

DYLAN: Did it?

GUSSIE: Wanna know how you got the name Dylan?

DYLAN: No.

GUSSIE: One night before you were born, we were partying . . . getting drunk. I had sold the Harley . . . I wish I hadn't sold that Harley.

DYLAN: Dad—

GUSSIE: It must of been around '72. Yeah. Because this is after Woodstock. And we're crazy, you know? Making no bread. Living month to month downstairs from this alcoholic transvestite. My hair's down to here. So we get wasted, we get wasted. Oh yeah. And we're singing "Like a Rolling Stone"—never forget that song. And I'm dancing around with Terence—he wasn't more than six months old— being silly. And I slipped and he hit his head on the edge of the table. Knocked him unconscious, blood was coming out of his nose.

DYLAN: You hit his head? No wonder.

GUSSIE: We freaked *out*, man. One minute we're laughing, the next minute, Terence is like a limp rabbit in my hands. I'm thinking, I killed my son! Michelle's calm. Just says one word: "Hospital."

DYLAN: Dad—

GUSSIE: Man. So we run out to our shitbox car—it won't start. The Rambler, you remember the Rambler? I'm swearing, I'm praying. We finally get to the hospital and—we don't have any money, Dylan. Don't even have a credit card. Have to wait six hours to see a doctor. Waiting room is filled with drunk people and screaming kids. Terence finally wakes up. He's crying. I keep rocking him. Dried blood all around his little nose . . . but no one cared. No one but your mother and me. And I vowed that night: Never again.

DYLAN: What does any of that have to do with my name?

GUSSIE: I realized something that night, Dylan. In the middle of all this "do your own thing" stuff, I wanted a life. A real life. Lemme tell you something about money, Dylan. *Money solves problems.* You can be some wild guy, with no goals, no aim. I remember one Christmas—

DYLAN: Dad, your meat is getting cold.

GUSSIE: Dylan, you guys are my life. If anything happened to you or your brother or Michelle, I don't know what I'd do.

DYLAN: So you named me Dylan?

GUSSIE: Yeah we named you Dylan, to remember what's important and what's not important.

DYLAN: Dad, none of that has anything to do with me.

GUSSIE: Don't let your mother find out about this. *(Reaches into his pocket and pulls out cash. Dylan takes it and walks off)*

(Tony, who has come outside to eat, has been listening.)

TONY: Great meat, Gus.

GUSSIE: You know, Tony, I look at that barbecue, and I have to laugh. Five grand. No big deal. I put it on the plastic. When Michelle and I bought our first house, the *down payment* was five grand. We'd lie awake nights trying to figure out how we were ever going to pay the mortgage. Four hundred a month. Spit.

TONY *(Chewing, his mouth full)*: Chump change.

GUSSIE: Twenty-five years later, and here we are. On top of the world.

TONY: A fucking accomplishment.

GUSSIE: That's right. And I did it by myself. No help from anyone, man.

TONY: That's because you got guts.

GUSSIE: That's right. I'd never say this in front of Michelle, but it took balls.

TONY: Big balls.

GUSSIE: And I can say to you: "My house is your house, Tony." I don't care who you are or where you've been. What you've done with your life. How you got your hands dirty. I don't care if you're the biggest loser in the world: "*Mi casa es su casa.*"

TONY: *Gracias.*

GUSSIE: It's karma, Tony. But you make your karma. Guys I knew went to Vietnam, came back in pieces. Came back in body bags. I could've gone. But I didn't because I was smart. You know what I mean? So I told 'em I was gay and they 4-F'd me. Let's face it, it's survival of the fittest *and* the smartest.

TONY: You're smarter than me.

(Gussie skewers a huge bell pepper and holds it up.)

GUSSIE: Look at this pepper. This is a perfect pepper. $8.50 a pound at Balducci's. But worth it. Because it's the *best*. Because I fucking deserve it.

(Gussie holds a basting brush in one hand and the skewered pepper in the other. He sings:)

What a long strange trip it's been . . .

(Gussie takes the bowl of peppers and onions and goes inside. Tony watches him go, then scratches his balls.
  Dylan reappears. He sits, waiting for Tony to go.)

TONY: You got any smoke? I could use a fat doobie right now.

DYLAN: I don't smoke pot. I don't drink.

(Roz comes out and starts searching under chairs, etc.)

TONY: Your brother is a lucky guy. Ever wonder why some people get all the breaks?

DYLAN: No.

TONY: Neither do I. I want something, I take it.

(Roz is not paying attention to the conversation.)

ROZ: Have you seen Jeremy's Tevas? Oh, never mind, here they are.

TONY *(To Dylan)*: You know what I'm saying?

DYLAN *(To Tony)*: I don't want anything, so it's not a problem I have to deal with.

TONY: Then you don't have a problem. I'm gonna get some more meat.

(Tony goes into the house.)

ROZ *(To Dylan)*: Aren't you eating?

DYLAN: On a diet.

ROZ: You should eat. You'll feel better.

DYLAN: Maybe I don't want to feel better.

ROZ: You're isolating. You're living in the problem.

(Roz comes close, on her way into the house.)

DYLAN: Yeah? Maybe I should put some "gratitude into my attitude."

ROZ: Maybe you should stop feeling sorry for yourself.

DYLAN: Yeah, I'll just have to build a mansion surrounded with trees. Roll out the old tatami mat on my polished floors and meditate.

ROZ: Oh, you don't have to unroll it.

DYLAN: No?

ROZ: No, keep it rolled up nice and tight, then you can shove it up your ass.

(Roz walks away.)

DYLAN: Can I ask you a quick question, Roz?

(Roz keeps walking.)

What's more fun, spending money or sucking my brother's dick?

(Roz turns to him.)

ROZ: You are one bitter motherfucker, aren't you? Sad and bitter.

DYLAN: I'm just trying to figure out how somebody as smart and together as you decides to waste her life as a prostitute-slash-babymaker for a cell phone slinging, rock climbing, cigar smoking, asswipe like my brother?

ROZ: I like the challenge.

DYLAN: You know, before we met I used to check you out in the lingerie catalogs, scope out your Wonderbra and sheer, see-through panties. I'd get out the Oil of Olay and shoot the moon, so to speak. I was obsessed. And it wasn't because you were a fox, a hardbody. It was that *look* in your eyes. The intelligence, the fierceness, that I was in love with. And then you started *dating Terence* and we'd all hang out and go dancing and drinking and I'd see you in the flesh and I'd say to myself, See? She's just like any other girl, she's no mystery.

But I never forgot that look of passion in your eyes.

(Roz moves in close to Dylan.)

ROZ: Wow. *(Beat)* You think you're special because you beat off to my picture, Dylan? Dude, I get *fan mail.*

(Dylan places his hand on her breast.)

DYLAN: I'm more than a fan. And you know it.

(Pause.)

ROZ: Yeah?

DYLAN: Yeah.

ROZ: I'll keep that in mind, stud. *(Moves away)*

DYLAN: You're a bimbo! You're white-bread! You're Barbie! Worse. You're a coward. *(Roz turns to face him)* Let's get naked. In front of everybody. Just strip down and fuck like dogs next to my dad's griller. Make one fucking moment count.

(Roz smiles, the thought appeals to her.)

ROZ: Yeah, man! And then we can all go get a tattoo!

DYLAN: I see the way you look at me.

ROZ: And what are you going to do about it, Dylan? Nothing.

(Dylan takes a step toward her, grabs her and kisses her. Long, long kiss. Finally, they pull apart.)

This is not a good idea.

(Tony, more food on his plate, has come outside and stands watching. He passes Roz as she goes into the house.)

DYLAN: S'matter, you don't like it inside?

TONY: Beautiful day like this, and they're afraid of flies. Hell, I *love* flies. *(Loud burp)*

(Face-off. Stare down.
  Jeremy enters eating a hot dog.)

JEREMY: Can I go swimming, Uncle Dylan?

TONY: Go in. I'll watch you.

(Dylan stays focused on Tony as Jeremy goes off to the pool.)

DYLAN: Whose uncle are you anyway?

TONY: No one's. It's a term of endearment.

DYLAN: We're not related?

JEREMY *(Off)*: Uncle Dylan, watch me float!!!

TONY: You heard the story.

DYLAN: About you saving my grampa's life?

TONY: That's the story. *(Sips his drink)* Not the whole story though.

DYLAN: Korea, right?

TONY: Our PT boat got hit by a mortar. We started to sink in the middle of this stinking river. Your grampa and me grabbed the same one-man lifeboat. They call it a "one-man" because only one man can use it or it sinks. I told Poppa to swim off 'cause we were both gonna drown. But he refused.

DYLAN: He refused?

(Jeremy screaming offstage.)

TONY: Stubborn bastard. So I faked being too tired to hold on and I sank underwater. Then I pulled a knife outta my boot and I was gonna gut him like a codfish when a rescue boat came along, saved us both. Everyone thinks I was going to sacrifice my life for his. He was so guilty. He introduced me to your granma, made me one of the family.

JEREMY *(Off)*: Uncle Dylan! Uncle Dylan, save me, I'm drowning!!! *(Beat)* There's a huge octopus pulling me under!

DYLAN: Dad says you're with the CIA.

TONY: I do what I have to do.

DYLAN: Yeah, me too.

(Dylan takes out a syringe, a bag of heroin and a bottlecap. He steals some water from the cooler and cooks it up. Tony takes his plate of meat over to the griller. Turns on the griller.)

TONY: I knew a guy in the navy. Junkie. Wore long sleeve shirts on hot days, just like you. Guy was a dreamer. Said he had to see the world so he could write about it. Said all the great

American writers went to sea. Got so high, he fell overboard in a storm. Nobody noticed. And nobody ever read a word he wrote.

(Tony puts his meat on the griller.)

He who hesitates is lost.

(This freezes Dylan. Tony attends to his meat.)

And goes hungry. These are the rules: Eat or be eaten; kill or be killed.

(Tony puts his hand inside the griller. He winces as a whiff of smoke drifts out. He removes his hand—grill marks have branded his palm. He reveals his hand to Dylan.)

Sink or swim, baby. Fish or cut bait.

(Angry, Dylan finally breaks his trance and shoots up. Long pause. Then he loosens the tie, and rests, the syringe still in his arm. Tony watches him benevolently.
    Long scream from Jeremy offstage.
    Blackout.)

ACT TWO

Dylan, alone, lies on the lawn with his eyes closed. He's got little stereo speakers perched next to his head. Nirvana's "Rape Me" plays.

Gussie and Tony emerge from the house, each holding a cigar and a glass of brandy.

GUSSIE: Fifteen thousand bucks. Nothing gets past it. "Armed response." Twenty-four hours a day. Trip that alarm, you don't know the password? Those guys show up and they shoot you, that's it. That's security. It's expensive, but fuck it, what else am I going to spend the money on?

(Gussie and Tony have made their way to the pool. They look at it together.)

It's weird. I'm the guy who lived in the same pair of jeans for five years. I don't *need* money. But it comes, and after a certain point I'm *forced* to spend it. And the funny thing is, aging hippie that I am, I *like* spending money. I *like* buying stuff. *Having* stuff. I like to look around at my stuff and think, I can afford all this shit.

TONY: You enjoy your success.

GUSSIE: You *have to* enjoy it. Half the world is starving to death, Tony! Some fucker in Bombay would give his right eye to live the way I live—*dreams* of living this life. So for me to not enjoy my life is like I'm letting that guy in Bombay down.

(Tony begins to strip off his clothes.)

See that water? Under Michelle's tennis court, I have a machine. Filters the pool five times an hour through imported sand. From the Canary Islands. Takes the water drop by drop, *electrocutes* it. Pure. Sterile. In nature, they don't have water this clean.

(Tony is now naked. He farts loudly and jumps into the pool.)

Jeez, Tony, if you didn't bring a suit, I would have been happy to lend you one.

(Michelle enters the yard, ready to set the table.)

MICHELLE: Who's having coffee? Gloria?

GLORIA *(Off)*: Coffee!

ROZ *(Off)*: Decaf!

(Terence enters, on his cell phone, as Michelle fusses over the table.)

TERENCE *(Into phone)*: No. No. No, don't do this to me, Dieter, c'mon. You're fucking me, man, you're killing me, you're raping me! Call me back. OK. OK. *(Ends call)*

(Gussie collects his barbecue tools and takes them inside. Terence watches Tony in the pool.)

Ma, Uncle Tony's swimming in the nude.

MICHELLE *(Glances up)*: He's not nude.

TERENCE: He is. Look.

(Michelle keeps her eyes down, setting the table.)

MICHELLE: Help me with this.

(Terence helps her.)

Your father and I were up pretty late last night with our own little celebration. By the time I fell asleep it was almost one A.M. You know how it is, old dogs take a little longer to shake hands.

TERENCE: "Old dogs"?

MICHELLE: I guess it's time to get the little blue pill. I mean he's not impotent or anything like that, he just doesn't have the concentration he used to have.

TERENCE *(Almost wincing)*: Ma!

MICHELLE: I'm not saying sex isn't good. In many ways, it's better. Much better. Slower, more sensual. And the big "O" is bigger. Deeper. Much deeper.

TERENCE: Ma, you're grossing me out.

MICHELLE: What do you think of me getting my belly button pierced?

GLORIA *(Off)*: Michelle, where's the heavy cream?

MICHELLE: Wait, you'll never find it!

(Michelle goes into the house. Terence watches Tony swim. He ambles down to Dylan and watches him "sleep.")

TERENCE *(Softly)*: Dylan. *(Louder)* Dylan. *(Louder)* Dylan!

(Dylan's eyes open.)

Dylan, what are you doing?

DYLAN: Resting.

TERENCE: You want to throw the ball around?

DYLAN: "Throw the ball around?"

TERENCE: We haven't thrown the ball around for a long time, man.

DYLAN: What ball? What the fuck are you talking about?

(Dylan sits up and finds a cigarette and lights it.)

Fuck, Terence. I was resting!

TERENCE: Dylan, if you were me, you know, had the kind of money I have, what would you do?

DYLAN: Do with what?

TERENCE: How would you spend it?

DYLAN: I'd buy a desert island. Far away. No phones, no cable, no people, no family.

TERENCE: But you need people. I mean people—what else is there?

DYLAN: I don't need people.

TERENCE: Well you need a woman in your life.

DYLAN: You think?

GLORIA *(Off)*: What about the cake?

MICHELLE *(Off)*: The cake!

TERENCE: Do you hate me, Dylan?

DYLAN: Why should I hate you? You're my brother.

TERENCE: Sometimes you sound like you hate me.

DYLAN *(Ironic)*: Maybe I do hate you. Wait. Come to think of it, yeah, I do.

TERENCE: That's what I thought. So . . . you need any money?

DYLAN: When you went to business school, did you take a special course on how to be an asshole? Because you are incredibly skilled.

TERENCE: I'm trying to have a normal conversation with you and you persist with this holier-than-thou victim shit. Like with that homeless guy. Like you have some higher purpose and I'm just this stupid worker ant, this materialistic dog.

DYLAN: Yeah, but Terence, you *are* those things.

TERENCE: And you know what *you* are? The grasshopper. I'm the ant and you're the grasshopper. Winter's coming pal, and I'm getting ready. You're not.

DYLAN: Terence, I'm walking down my path, you walk down yours. I don't give a shit.

TERENCE: Oh yeah? You're so smart. Above it all. You think I want to be here? No. But I have a responsibility to Mom and Dad.

DYLAN: I'm here just like you.

TERENCE: So everyone can see how you're suffering. Feel your pain. You could never live on a desert island, there'd be nobody around to watch you be a martyr.

(Terence walks off. Dylan watches Tony swim.

Michelle brings out a large birthday cake in the shape of the Eiffel Tower. She is followed by Roz and Gloria, who carry pastries, etc.)

MICHELLE: It's kind of corny, but I like it.

ROZ: It's very cool.

GLORIA: Is it supposed to be something?

MICHELLE: The Eiffel Tower!

(Tony emerges from the water, naked, dripping. He wraps a towel around himself.)

I better go get the candles.

GLORIA: I better help you.

(Michelle and Gloria go into the house. Roz, unfazed by Tony's nudity, stays behind. Tony finishes drying off and slips his clothes on. Dylan lies inert on the ground.)

TONY: You should have tried the meat.

ROZ: Meat is bad karma. Keeping those poor animals in bondage, force-feeding them, torturing them with electric shocks, slashing their throats, just so we can have a barbecue! I saw a TV show about what we do to pigs. How we kill them while they squeal and scream in horror. Factory farms are like bacon-burger concentration camps.

TONY: When people get hungry, someone's got to get their hands bloody.

(Dylan gets up and walks off. Roz watches him go.)

ROZ: You're a soldier. That's your thing, I guess.

TONY: Haven't done much soldiering for a long time. Now it's all corporate work. Oil, bananas, coffee.

ROZ: Were you in Vietnam?

TONY: Sure, Korea, Vietnam, El Salvador, Baghdad, Sierra Leone, Haiti—been to a lot of places. Thailand.

ROZ: Oh, that's right, you said I reminded you of your Ping-Pong partner.

TONY: Toi-Mai—petite little thing—danced in a club in Pattaya. She'd stand on the bar and strip, stuff herself with Ping-Pong balls, squat, pop 'em right into my glass of beer.

(He gazes at Roz.)

ROZ: Hmmm, I wouldn't have pegged you for a strip-club kind of guy. So you like that perverted stuff, huh?

TONY: Sure. Just like you like strutting around half naked, cock-teasing every man you meet.

ROZ: Hey, I can't help what goes on inside the twisted mind of an old fuck like you.

TONY: You calling me an old fuck?

ROZ *(Laughs)*: Yeah, I am. A funny old fuck.

(Tony laughs with her. They laugh together. Then suddenly Tony stops laughing.)

TONY *(Very somber)*: I'll give you an old fuck. And it won't be funny. I'll even teach you to do tricks.

ROZ: You don't scare me. Before I met Terence I worked with coked-up photographers who'd lay all that scary shit on me. Think they were Satan or something.

TONY: Maybe they were. You never know. How many did you screw? Ten? Twenty? Fifty?

ROZ *(Tense)*: Look, "Uncle Tony," I didn't do anything to you. So back off. OK?

(Tony laughs, breaking the tension.)

TONY: Roz, you don't eat meat, you don't like Ping-Pong. You're covered with sunblock. I didn't think you'd be so . . . careful. Young girl like you. Guess I had you all wrong.

ROZ: Guess you did.

TONY: I thought you wanted more out of life. Big girl like you, I'd think you'd have more of an appetite.

(He comes up behind her.)

Why are you holding back? Why are you denying yourself? You only live once.

ROZ: Terence takes care of me very well. Believe me. I have everything I want.

TONY: Sure you do. Every house-pet thinks it's happy.

JEREMY *(Off)*: MOMMY! MOMMY! MOMMY!

(Jeremy comes tearing in from the house.)

ROZ: Go find Daddy, he's got something for you.

(Jeremy leaves. Roz looks back at Tony.)

TONY: "Freedom's just another word for nothing left to lose . . ."

ROZ: Hey, fuck off!

(Roz walks off.

Tony sits in a recliner—the picture of contentment. Gussie and Michelle come out of the house, followed by Gloria.)

GUSSIE: Gloria, you're getting hysterical. I'll call *my* doctor on Monday, see what *he* says.

GLORIA: I'm telling you. They have a test now, they know she has cancer, they just don't know where.

GUSSIE: Great test.

MICHELLE: Have they told her?

GLORIA: No one's saying anything until I figure out what I'm going to do.

MICHELLE: Gloria, I know an excellent acupuncturist. Cured my spider veins—$60.00 a vein.

GLORIA: Acupuncture isn't going to fix this! Besides, it's the whole thing.

MICHELLE: What "thing"?

GLORIA: Afterwards, in the house, chemotherapy, running around. Even if she doesn't . . . die, I don't want to deal with it. *(Resolute)* I'm putting her in a *place*. They can take care of her better there.

MICHELLE: You want her to leave the house?

GLORIA: Well, I haven't said anything yet.

MICHELLE: It's *her* house.

GLORIA: Legally it's mine. The lawyer had her sign it over to me five years ago.

GUSSIE: OK, you're getting way ahead of yourself here.

GLORIA: You don't have to *live* with her, Gus! Last week she wakes me up at three in the morning, she can't remember the name of an actor in *Route 66*.

GUSSIE: George Maharis.

GLORIA: No, the other one. Now *I* can't remember. Look, the doctors say—

GUSSIE *(Thinking)***:** Oh Jeez . . . It's . . . Mark—

MICHELLE: Not Mark, uh, Martin—

GUSSIE: Right . . . Martin Milner.

(Relief all around at getting that straight.)

GLORIA: Gus, I'm not joking now! You know what? You don't want her to go in a home, she can live here.

GUSSIE: She can't live here.

GLORIA: Why not?

GUSSIE: Don't you love your mother?

MICHELLE: Gus!

GLORIA: I've seen other people go through it and I can't do it, *Gus.* I'm already at my limit. I'm not going to start changing diapers!

GUSSIE: Wait! Gloria, how much is this place going to cost? Who's going to pay for it? Have you thought about that? If something happens to her in there, how are you going to feel? *(To Michelle)* She never thinks things through.

GLORIA: Gussie.

GUSSIE: You're not putting her in a home. We'll work something out. Just not right now. Please.

GLORIA: Gussie.

GUSSIE *(To Michelle)***:** Is the coffee ready?

(Gloria picks up a magazine and starts reading. Tony leans farther back in the recliner.)

My sister loves to drop things in my lap.

MICHELLE: Betty's not living here, Gus. I don't need any more children in this house.

GUSSIE: This is my mother, for God's sake. What am I supposed to do?

MICHELLE: And I'm your wife. And I'm telling you.

GUSSIE: I'll check on the coffee.

(Gussie goes into the house as Terence returns.)

TERENCE: Where's Dad going?

MICHELLE: He's gone to check on the coffee.

TERENCE: The coffee's not made?

MICHELLE: Not yet.

TERENCE: How can we have dessert if the coffee's not made?

MICHELLE: Terence, some days Mommy doesn't have all the answers.

(Michelle goes into the house. Jeremy zooms in and grabs Terence's hand.)

JEREMY: Daddy, let's go look for birds' nests!

(He starts to drag Terence out.)

TERENCE: Where'd Roz go?

(No answer. Terence and Jeremy exit.)

TONY: Is it time for dessert?

GLORIA: Would I be sitting here? *(Indicating the magazine)* See this picture, this man? He's very smart. I heard him speak the other night in person.

TONY: Yeah?

GLORIA: It was very interesting. Did you know that by the year 2010 most people in this country won't be able to speak English? Most people won't even be *white*. I mean, I have nothing against those people, or whatever, but you know, this is a white country. This guy was talking about a race war.

TONY: There's a place out in some woods I own. I have this hole I dug.

GLORIA: Hole?

TONY: Bunker, like a bomb shelter. You know what I got in that hole? Freeze-dried food, water, gasoline in a drum. Shotgun. Couple of M-16's. Plastique. Grenades. Trip wire.

GLORIA: Yeah, right. You don't. *(Curious)* Really?

TONY: Everyone should have a hole.

GLORIA: Well, I'm trying to get out of mine.

TONY: I think you don't give yourself credit.

GLORIA: Me neither.

TONY: No, I mean, here you are, a woman in the prime of her life, very alive. Passionate. Intelligent.

GLORIA: It's funny that you say that, because I was just thinking yesterday people treat me like a pushover, but I'm not. I'm really not.

TONY: You're the backbone of the family. And you're not appreciated.

GLORIA: Well, that's right.

TONY: Where would they be without you?

GLORIA: That's right. And that's what this guy was saying at the meeting. You have to stand up for what you believe. Stop taking it.

TONY: I agree.

GLORIA: My mother thinks I can't make decisions. I'm forty-eight years old. I've been making decisions my whole life! Yesterday a real-estate woman called, wanted to know if she could come by to look at the house. I said I'd think about it. My mother won't let me call her back. I'd say it's up to me who I call and who I don't call.

TONY: I agree.

GLORIA: You do?

TONY: Of course.

GLORIA: Well, that means a lot to me, because I respect your opinion. Poppa's friend and everything.

TONY: I've known you since you were a little girl. Your dad would come by the club, late afternoon. And you'd be holding his hand. He was so proud of you.

GLORIA: Yeah. I remember the club. Cigar smoke. Drunk guys handing me Chiclets, pinching my cheek. You were there, too?

TONY: Sure. He'd buy you a Shirley Temple, let you play the jukebox: Three Dog Night. He'd say, "This is not my little girl. This is the woman in my life."

(Gloria is getting sucked into the memory.)

GLORIA: He used to say that.

TONY: I'd be jealous. A bachelor, no kids. A pretty little girl like you. You were such a pretty little thing. What could be nicer?

GLORIA: He wouldn't take Gus to the club. He was afraid Gus would be corrupted. He'd just take me.

TONY: To show you off. Because he was proud of you.

GLORIA: He was.

(Gloria starts to sniffle. Tony lets it sink in.)

TONY: Hey. He was a great guy.

GLORIA *(Holding back tears)*: He was my daddy.

TONY: We all miss him.

GLORIA: Things were never the same after he died.

(Tony goes to Gloria and puts his arms around her. He strokes her hair.)

TONY: Hey.

(He lifts her up. They stand in an embrace. Gloria closes her eyes and Tony holds her for a while. Then they start to slow dance. Tony caresses her bum very, very gently.)

This feels good, doesn't it?

(Gloria gets into it, forgetting where she is. She nuzzles into Tony, maybe coos a bit. Tony puts a hand under her blouse. Gloria's losing it.

She pulls away, confused.)

Jesus, Gloria, you're all grown up!

(Flustered, Gloria grabs her pocketbook and walks off. Tony grabs the bottle of whiskey, wanders to a chair, sits down and pours himself a drink. Michelle emerges and flutters around the food. She sees Tony drinking, as she predicted, but tries to be civil.)

MICHELLE: How does everything look?

TONY: Beautiful. The table is beautiful, the yard is beautiful and you're beautiful.

MICHELLE: Uh-huh.

(Michelle takes his bottle of whiskey and recaps it. She eyes the table and sips her wine.)

TONY: When's Betty moving in?

MICHELLE: She's not!

TONY: I don't blame you. I had to put a dog down once. It was no fun. No fun at all.

MICHELLE: She's not dying. We honestly don't have the room.

TONY: Ah, come on! She's creepy and she's a drag. She doesn't even smell that good.

MICHELLE: Tony!

TONY: "Those not busy being born are busy dying."

MICHELLE: You listen to Dylan?

TONY: Let's go out to the gazebo and screw.

MICHELLE: You really know how to flatter a girl.

TONY: I'm completely serious.

MICHELLE: Yeah? *(Can't meet his eyes)* Thanks. I'm married.

TONY: So to speak.

MICHELLE: You're drunk.

TONY: Right. You're absolutely right. Look, you got a lot to do. Go ahead. I'll watch the cake.

(Michelle goes into the house. As soon as she's gone, Tony runs his finger in the frosting. Eats some. Jeremy bops in, almost catches Tony fingering the cake.)

JEREMY: What are you doing?

TONY: Taste testing.

JEREMY: You're not supposed to do that.

TONY: Oh, there's lots of things you're not supposed to do. Where's your daddy?

JEREMY: Looking for Mommy.

(Jeremy watches Tony suck down more frosting, transfixed by this sin.)

I'm going out to L.A. I'm going to be a big star. Everyone says.

TONY: I know some people out there. I'll hook you up.

JEREMY: You will?

(Tony lifts Jeremy onto his lap. Tony scoops frosting onto his finger and holds it under Jeremy's nose.)

TONY: Sure. I'll give 'em your name. They're always looking for fresh talent.

(Jeremy licks Tony's finger as Roz enters. Her hair is mussed. She sees Jeremy on Tony's lap. She pours herself a shot of whiskey.)

ROZ: Where's Daddy?

(Roz lifts Jeremy off Tony's lap and puts him in a chair.)

JEREMY: He's looking for you.

ROZ: Yeah?

JEREMY: Don't be an alcoholic like Uncle Dylan! I'll tell Daddy.

ROZ: That's a good idea. Go tell Daddy, Mommy's decided to become an alcoholic.

JEREMY *(Running off)*: DADDY! DADDY!!

(Tony runs his fingers through the frosting and licks them.)

ROZ: That's the birthday cake.

TONY: I know. I'm guarding it.

> *(Tony takes another lick. Roz laughs, pours another shot.)*

Try some.

ROZ: I don't think frosting and whiskey mix.

TONY: Sure they do.

> *(Roz runs a finger across the frosting. Licks it.)*

ROZ: It's good. Ummmm.

> *(Roz steals another bite.)*

We're being bad.

TONY: Uh-oh!!! We're in trouble now! How's Dylan?

ROZ: He has a lot of energy when he feels like it.

TONY: I bet.

> *(Roz smooths her hair, adjusts her swimsuit in the crotch.)*

ROZ: God! I wish everything was as easy as frosting.

> *(Tony laughs, Roz giggles. Gussie enters from the kitchen. Jeremy tags after him.)*

GUSSIE: Coffee's ready in five minutes.

> *(Gussie sees the damage to the cake. The top has been eaten off.)*

Hey! What happened to my cake? Jeremy?

JEREMY: I didn't do anything. It was—

ROZ: I promised Jeremy we'd roast marshmallows.

JEREMY: Yeah!

GUSSIE: On what?

ROZ: On your griller.

GUSSIE: No, no, no, no, no. The stuff melts, and—

(Granma Betty enters, and goes for Jeremy.)

GRANMA BETTY: *Five* James Bonds. Sean Connery, Roger Moore, Pierce Brosnan, George Lazenby and there's one more . . . Timothy Dalton. You owe me five bucks. And I'm not taking a check.

TERENCE *(Off)*: MA! DAD!

(Jeremy goes to the griller and pushes the button to turn it on.)

GUSSIE: Don't push that, Jeremy.

TERENCE *(Off)*: DAD!

GUSSIE: What's Terence shouting about?

(Gloria and Michelle enter.)

MICHELLE: Coffee's ready everybody!

GUSSIE: No. Wait a sec . . . Terence . . .

MICHELLE *(Sees the cake)*: What happened here!!! Jeremy!

(Terence enters, dragging Dylan by his collar.)

TERENCE: The fuck is going on here?

DYLAN: What?

(Terence holds a joint in front of Dylan's nose.)

TERENCE: What is this?

DYLAN: No idea.

TERENCE: You don't know?!!

DYLAN: Um, a toothpick? A life-size model of your dick?

TERENCE: It's a *joint*. Marijuana. Pot.

GUSSIE: What's going on?

(Dylan finds himself at the griller, surrounded, people everywhere.)

JEREMY: Was Uncle Dylan getting high?

GUSSIE: He's drunk again?

TERENCE: No, it's more than that. It's more than that, Dad.

DYLAN: You're such a jerk. You know that? An unredeemable jerk.

GUSSIE: Wait a minute now! Are you all right, Dylan?

DYLAN: Like you give a flying fuck! You buy my paintings, you don't hang them up. You don't even have the decency to hang them up when I'm here.

MICHELLE: That's so wrong, Dylan, I have one of your paintings . . . right in the front hall where people come in.

GUSSIE: I took it down.

DYLAN: You know, there's a million places I could be today. But I show up here, because I need the money. I show up. And then you make me beg from you. Like a little dog. Like a little trained dog.

GUSSIE: Is he delirious?

DYLAN: A HUNDRED BUCKS HERE, A HUNDRED BUCKS THERE! "DON'T TELL YOUR MOTHER." "DON'T TELL YOUR FATHER." I'M LIKE SOME KIND OF MID-PRICED HOOKER. IF YOU REALLY LOVED ME YOU'D GIVE ME ENOUGH SO I COULD LIVE LIKE A HUMAN BEING. YOU EVER THINK MAYBE I WANT A BMW TOO? I'M YOUR FUCK-ING SON!!! YOU'VE SPENT MORE MONEY ON THAT FUCKING POOL THAN YOU'VE EVER SPENT ON ME.

GUSSIE: That's completely untrue.

MICHELLE: *Gus.* —Terence, why do you have to start these things?

TERENCE: *Me?*

DYLAN: Look at us. Pretending we're a family. Acting our parts so that if anybody asks us we can say things like, "Yeah, I have a mother." "Yeah, I have a son. I love him *so much*!"

MICHELLE: I don't know what's bothering you, Dylan, but why don't you go inside and cool off?

DYLAN: Just 'cause you say something doesn't mean you mean it. Love is about sacrifice, about being unselfish. Being there for someone. But you could never do that, because you can't get past your own little playpen, in which I am simply one more toy. Every time I hear my own fucking name I think, My own father couldn't be bothered giving me a real name!

TERENCE: He's trying to change the subject.

MICHELLE: We do love you, Dylan.

DYLAN: No you don't. I'm just something you two excreted.

GUSSIE: Did your therapist tell you to say all this? I've told you again and again.

DYLAN: Yeah. You *told* me. You never stop telling me.

(Dylan leans onto the red-hot griller.)

OWWWWWW!!!! SHIT!!!

(Dylan kicks the griller.)

GUSSIE: Hey!

(Roz rushes over and takes hold of his hand.)

ROZ: What'd you do??? Burn your hand?

TERENCE: Jesus H. Christ!

GUSSIE: Get him in the house, put some water on it.

MICHELLE: I got it, Gussie, I got it. Ice cubes.

GRANMA BETTY: Butter, put butter on it.

(Dylan is hustled into the kitchen by Michelle and Roz, followed by Jeremy. Terence gets a beer. Gussie finds Dylan's cigarettes and lights one. Tony stays by the cake, drinking.)

GUSSIE: Terence, why do you have to start all this shit?

TERENCE: You think I *want* to find his stash? I don't want him back in the rehab! I take any more time off for family counseling I'll start losing accounts.

(Michelle emerges from the house.)

How's the junkie?

MICHELLE: He went upstairs with Roz to put something on his hand. Don't call your brother that.

(Gussie starts taking the griller apart, fastidiously cleaning it.)

TERENCE: You used to smoke pot in the old days. You think it's revolutionary to get stoned. An act of rebellion against "the man"! Mr. Liberal.

GUSSIE: I'm not liberal about anything.

TERENCE: You've protected him his whole life. That's why he's so fucked-up.

MICHELLE: No one's protecting anybody.

TERENCE: Ma, I know you're giving him money.

MICHELLE: Who?

GUSSIE: What money?

MICHELLE: Money isn't everything, Terence.

TERENCE: Yes it is! *Of course* it is! You think I work so hard because I *like* to? So you can turn around and give this *junkie* a free ride? He's a leech, a parasite. Why don't you admit your son's a parasite?

(Jeremy enters, shuffling his feet.)

GRANMA BETTY: Leave Dylan alone, he's sowing his wild oats.

MICHELLE: Granma Betty, have a madeleine!

GRANMA BETTY: If Gloria can spare one.

MICHELLE: OK. Everything will be fine. Dylan's going through a confusing period.

JEREMY *(Glazed)*: Daddy, I don't want to watch any more TV.

TERENCE *(Gentle)*: You don't? Well, what *do* you want to do?

JEREMY: Stay out here where it's interesting.

TERENCE: Where's Mommy?

JEREMY: She's upstairs with Uncle Dylan. The door's locked. And they won't let me in.

TERENCE: Listen, honey, go in and watch until the next commercial, and then we'll go look at the fireworks.

JEREMY *(Excited)*: We will?

TERENCE: Uh-huh. Now go back in—

JEREMY: Fireworks! Fireworks! Fireworks! *(Goes inside)*

GUSSIE *(To Michelle)*: What money?

TERENCE *(Up to the window)*: Roz! *Roz!*

(Pause. Gussie works steadily, cleaning his griller.)

MICHELLE: Granma, would you like some coffee?

GRANMA BETTY: Is it instant?

MICHELLE: Of course not!

GUSSIE: There's a scratch on the side here, see that scratch?

TERENCE: When he's dead from an overdose, you won't be thinking about your griller. We should stick him in a rehab and throw away the key.

GUSSIE: You're being way too dramatic.

MICHELLE: Gloria, you haven't said anything.

GLORIA: You want *me* to say something?

MICHELLE: He is your nephew.

GLORIA: I think—

(Roz enters.)

ROZ: He's okay. He'll be down in a minute.

(Michelle exits.)

TERENCE: What were you doing up there with him all this time?

ROZ: Giving him a urine test.

(Jeremy returns; goes to Terence.)

JEREMY: Daddy, can we go to the fireworks now?

TERENCE: NOT NOW, Jeremy! Go to Mommy. She has something for you.

JEREMY: Daddy never does what he says he's going to do.

GLORIA: I was saying—

GUSSIE: Have another madeleine, Gloria.

GLORIA: I don't want another madeleine. I was saying something, but I guess no one really cares what I have to say, so I won't say it.

GUSSIE: Gloria, what? Spit it out!

GRANMA BETTY: Let her eat. She doesn't want to talk, she wants to eat.

(Long pause.)

GLORIA: I've sold the house. Twenty minutes ago. I just got an offer and I sold it.

GUSSIE: You sold the house?

TERENCE: Where's Granma going to live?

GLORIA: You have fourteen thousand square feet? Five hundred is all she needs. Keep her in the atrium. She can water the plants.

(Dylan, sporting a bandaged hand, bursts outside followed by Michelle.)

DYLAN: No! No way! No rehab. Not again.

MICHELLE: Dylan, just listen to your brother.

DYLAN: No. Forget it. Ain't happening.

TERENCE: What, you're gonna be a junkie the rest of your life?

DYLAN: What, you're gonna be a broker the rest of your life?

TERENCE: After everything Mom and Dad gave you. You're a dropout, you're jobless. Now you're a stoner good-for-nothing.

I can't think of anything you could do that could hurt them more.

DYLAN: You never had much of an imagination.

TONY: Fish or cut bait.

(Dylan walks over to Roz. Kisses her long and hard. She looks completely chagrined.)

ROZ: Shit!

GRANMA BETTY: Dylan, I didn't realize you were such a good kisser!

TERENCE: Leave her alone!

ROZ: It's OK, Terence.

TERENCE: No it's not!

MICHELLE: No one's eating these desserts.

GUSSIE: Michelle, we're having a little family crisis here.

(Terence looks back and forth between Dylan and Roz.)

TERENCE: What were you two doing in the bedroom?

ROZ: *Nothing.* God, you are so paranoid, Terence. Jeez!

(Dylan lights a cigarette, a big shit-eating grin on his face.)

DYLAN: Yeah, nothing's happened. Everything's cool.

ROZ *(Smiling):* Terence! Lighten up. He's pulling your chain!

MICHELLE: OK, OK, that's enough. Everyone calm down.

DYLAN: Wait, I forget, do blow jobs count?

(BOOM!!! Terence punches Dylan in the face.)

Shit!

(Terence is on him, pounding him on the ground.)

TERENCE: Little jerk, think you're so funny.

(Terence is vicious.)

DYLAN: Dude, you gotta cut down on the Viagra, it makes you tense.

(Terence stops.)

TERENCE *(To Roz)*: You told him?
ROZ: Of course not!

(Dylan laughs.)

DYLAN: Thirty-two and can't get it up. Pathetic.

(Terence resumes pummeling Dylan.)

ROZ: You're hurting him. Terence! Get off him!

(Roz runs to pull Terence off Dylan. Jeremy jumps in.)

JEREMY: Wrestling!!! Yay!

(Terence throws Jeremy off, keeps pounding Dylan.)

TERENCE: I GIVE HER EVERYTHING SHE WANTS. EVERY TIME I GET ANOTHER BONUS, LAND ANOTHER ACCOUNT, IT'S GONE FASTER THAN THE PLASTIC CAN SLIDE THROUGH THE MACHINE. I'M LIKE A HAMSTER ON A TREADMILL. I CAN NEVER STOP. THEN I COME HOME TO UNWIND, WATCH TV, DRINK A BEER, AND MY NYMPHOMANIAC WIFE WANTS LIVE PORNO.
ROZ: "Live porno"? What does *that* mean?
TERENCE: You want me to "take care of business." It's easy for you, you're a woman. You just lie there.
ROZ: Since when? When do I "lie there"?

MICHELLE: Gussie, do something for God's sake!

GUSSIE: Come on everyone, calm down!

ROZ: Pull it out right now, big guy, and show me how you're such a stud and I'm so passive.

(Terence stands up. He brushes himself off. Dylan lies there, fucked-up, moaning.)

TERENCE: Roz, shut up!

ROZ: Don't take *my* inventory, Terence. Don't go there, Mr. Softee!

GUSSIE: OK, OK, everybody, just relax. Just a little too much excitement. Everything's OK. Boy!

(Pause. Gloria speaks up.)

GLORIA: I'm moving away. *(Beat)* There's a place outside Denver. Run by this man I heard speak. He's a wonderful man. Very caring. He cares about me. I'm going to live there.

(Tony from his perch, cheers her on.)

TONY: Good for you, Gloria!

(Gloria avoids Tony's look.)

GUSSIE: Shhhh! Where?!

GLORIA: It's like a community. It *is* a community. Of white people. And I'm moving there.

MICHELLE *(Incredulous)*: But what are you going to live on, Gloria? You won't have a job!

GLORIA: They take care of you there. Once you join, you sign over your assets and you're taken care of. And I want to be taken care of. *(Angrier and angrier)* I'm tired of being the one who makes the beds and cleans the toilets and brings home a check and doesn't get a thing for it.

GRANMA BETTY: Gloria, have you been drinking?

GLORIA: No I have not been drinking! I have *never* been drinking. Or tripping. Or screwing. Or anything. Ever. I'm just a some kind of sterile workhorse. A mule. Soon as I close on the house I'm outta here.

MICHELLE *(Fixing candles on cake)*: Listen everybody, let's have Gussie's cake and then we can decide what's what. OK?

JEREMY: Yeah! Let's have cake!

GUSSIE: Yeah, what about my cake?

MICHELLE *(To everybody)*: We have to sing "Happy Birthday." That's what we're here for . . .

(Michelle lights the candles.)

(Muttering to herself) More the Leaning Tower of Pisa now, but . . . *(Brightly)* "Happy Birthday to you . . ." etc.

ALL: "Happy Birthday to you . . ."

JEREMY: Make a wish!

(Gussie does, then blows out the candles. The phone starts ringing, and Gloria heads for the kitchen.)

GLORIA: That's for me.

TERENCE *(To Roz)*: We have to talk.

ROZ: When we get home.

TERENCE: *Now.*

(Terence takes Roz's hand and pulls her off. Jeremy follows them. Michelle looks forlornly at all the food. Dylan walks off.)

MICHELLE: The cream!

(Michelle goes into the house, leaving Gussie, Tony and Granma Betty onstage.)

GUSSIE: What's that Chinese curse: "May you live through interesting times"? How's it go?

TONY: Shit happens.

GUSSIE: Shit happens.

(Gussie gravitates to his griller.)

Just want to have a little family barbecue, is that some
kind of sin? No TV, no shopping malls, no ski lifts, just us,
together in the backyard. Ma? Remember the apple tree?
We used to swing while Poppa cooked. That's all I wanted.
A day under the apple tree. With my sons, my wife. My
baby grandson. That's all. Is it *bad* to want that?

*(Tony picks up the joint and lights it, sucks noisily. He offers it
to Gussie.)*

TONY: Want some?

GUSSIE: What is that? The pot? Jesus, Tony! The last thing I need.

*(Gussie takes the joint, takes a hit, and hands it back to Tony.
Gussie cleans the griller.)*

TONY: It's good shit.

*(Tony offers the joint to Granma Betty. Not knowing what it is,
she takes a hit.)*

(Slightly stoned) That is one nice griller you have there, boy.

GRANMA BETTY: The meat was very good. *Very* good.

TONY: It was.

GRANMA BETTY: Almost as good as your father's.

(Tony pours a drink for Gussie, gives it to him.)

TONY: Gus, have a drink.

GUSSIE: No.

TONY: C'mon.

> *(Gussie knocks it back. Tony pours one for himself, knocks it back, then hands another to Gussie, who knocks it back. Now Tony hands the joint to Gussie, who, without thinking, takes another hit. Tony puts the bottle and the glass on the griller, then hands Granma Betty the joint. She takes it.)*

Atta boy. When in doubt, knock 'em out.

GRANMA BETTY: I'm gonna be a homeless person like those people on TV.

GUSSIE: Ma, please. Don't start.

GRANMA BETTY: Well, where am I gonna live? I don't have a house like you do.

GUSSIE: We'll figure something out.

GRANMA BETTY: What are you gonna figure out? You can't even figure out your own kids.

TONY: Have another drink, Gus.

> *(Tony gives Gussie another drink. He downs it.)*

GUSSIE: We'll get you a spot in front of the supermarket, Ma. You can ask people for spare change. Who could turn you down?

TONY *(Mock protest)*: Gus! Stop!

GUSSIE *(Relishing the image)*: Really, Ma. It could be a whole new life for you. I bet you'd really score. Sweet little old lady. You'd rake it in. You'd be rich. All the red wine you could drink. *Sweet.*

> *(Gussie's getting a little giddy. Tony is laughing along with him.)*

TONY: Gus, you're talking about your mother!

GUSSIE: She can handle it.

GRANMA BETTY: I'm scared.

GUSSIE: Don't be scared, Ma, come on. I'm pulling your leg. You think I'd let anything happen to you?

GRANMA BETTY: You'll put me in one of those Medicaid nursing homes.

GUSSIE: No I won't.

GRANMA BETTY: Yes you will.

GUSSIE: No I *won't*.

GRANMA BETTY: You will.

GUSSIE: I won't!

GRANMA BETTY: Right.

GUSSIE: Don't try to guilt me out, Ma. That stuff works with Gloria, it doesn't work with me.

GRANMA BETTY: Just put me wherever you want me.

GUSSIE: I don't want you anywhere, Ma. I just want you to be happy.

GRANMA BETTY: That's nice. And I want *you* to be happy.

GUSSIE: No, not what makes *me* happy. What makes *you* happy.

GRANMA BETTY: That's right.

GUSSIE: What?

GRANMA BETTY: What you just said.

GUSSIE: You're getting me angry, Ma. Just stop.

GRANMA BETTY: Why are you angry? Because *I* have to move out of my own house and live in a place that smells like piss and shit, and get bossed around by a bunch of underpaid immigrants and hang out all day with semi-demented old strangers? That makes *you* angry?

GUSSIE: You know what?

(Gussie grabs the cake, walks off and throws it into the pool. He reenters.)

Forget the cake. The cake's all wet.

(Michelle, as if on cue, appears with the pot of coffee.)

MICHELLE: Where's the cake?

GUSSIE: Floating in the pool.

TONY: I hope it doesn't clog up the Canary Island sand.

(Terence, Roz and Jeremy enter.)

TERENCE: Dad, we're gonna get going.

(Gloria enters from the house.)

GLORIA: It's all set. The agent thinks she can close by the end of the week.

GUSSIE: Gloria, wait a second . . .

GLORIA: No. No more waiting.

(Dylan enters from offstage, moving slowly and shakily. Jeremy skips off.)

DYLAN: Dad?

GUSSIE: Dylan, we're in the middle of something right now. Gimme five minutes. Gloria . . .

DYLAN: Dad.

MICHELLE: Gus, he's all green.

DYLAN: I'm sorry, Dad. *(To Roz)* I love you!

(Dylan stumbles, gets underneath the table, and curls into a fetal position.)

ROZ: Oh my God!

GLORIA: Why's Dylan under the table?

GUSSIE: Dylan, what are you doing under there? What's wrong? What's he doing, Michelle?

MICHELLE: I don't know, Gus. Dylan are you OK?

(Dylan starts retching, as Jeremy comes skipping in holding a syringe.)

JEREMY: Look what I found!

(Terence quickly takes the syringe from Jeremy.)

TERENCE: Give me that!
JEREMY: Daddy!
MICHELLE: Gus!

(But before Gussie can make it to the kitchen, Tony goes into action. He reaches under the table, grabs the limp Dylan by the scruff of the neck, and pulls him out onto the lawn.)

TONY: Worked hard for fifty years, and I think, Take a break, kick back. You deserve it. Find a nice sunny spot, have a drink, relax.

Never had time for a family, never had time for so many things. So I come here, to your house, to join in so to speak, but you know what? I don't find it relaxing. Not relaxing at all.

(Tony pulls Dylan's head back, bends down over him, and blows air into his lungs.)

In fact, I kind of have a headache. Or some kind of ache. Or pain. Pain in the ass. And the Bible says: "If thine eye offend thee, pluck it out." You know? Pluck it the fuck out. And that's the way it's always been for me. Everything falls on my shoulders. 'Cause guys like me, we can't relax. We feel responsible. If I relax, what happens to the world? It gets all fucked-up!

(SMACK! Tony slaps Dylan, and Dylan rouses slightly.)

What would you do without me?

(Dylan is intensely groggy as Tony lifts him, pulls his arm around his shoulders, and walks him around the yard.)

DYLAN: Where . . . ? Dad? Ma?

TONY: I'm always cleaning your messes. That's the story of my life.

(Tony lifts Dylan off the ground, walks him over to the pool and tosses him in. Splashing sounds.)

He'll be OK. It's good for him.

MICHELLE *(Shouting):* Dylan, are you all right?

(Dylan drags himself out of the pool and collapses. Gussie pushes past the group and embraces his shivering, coughing, saturated son.)

GUSSIE: It's OK, honey, it's OK. Daddy's here.

(Dylan throws up.)

TONY: Wasn't it Tolstoy who said: "All happy families resemble each other and each unhappy family is unhappy in its own way"? I sit here and can't figure out if you're happy or sad? And if you are sad, I can't figure out what you're so sad about.

(Tony finds a cigarette and lights it.)

One time, south of the border, I walked in on a real happy family. Walked in while they were chewing their rice and beans.

GUSSIE: Dylan, let's get you upstairs.

DYLAN: No, I gotta just sit here for a second.

TONY: My men stood to one side with their M-16s and I walked in. *"Buenas noches,"* I said. But the family, they didn't have anything to say. The father, he was a lot like you Gus, stood up, like he was going to do something. Then he just started crying. He had a boy. Must of been about eight years old, sitting at the table. I went over and stood behind the little gaucho, put one hand on his forehead, and with my free hand slit his little throat. But no one moved. No one did a thing about it. Something about being in the presence of an American-made automatic weapon really slows people down.

GUSSIE: Tony, we don't need this right now.

TONY: Then I did the daughter. Then the wife. The baby. One by one. This was in an official capacity, of course. Unofficial, official capacity. The father watched and he cried. What could he do? Afterwards my men cut their heads off and nailed them to that dinner table. A plate of rice and beans in front of each one.

(Gussie rocks Dylan in his arms.)

GUSSIE: It's going to be OK.

TONY: See, we were there to make a point, and we made it. You know how a dog pisses on a tree to mark it? That was my job. To make a mark for old Uncle Sam. So people would know we'd been there.

GUSSIE *(To Tony)*: Tony, party's over. Why don't you take your ugly stories and your ugly face and get the fuck out of my backyard?

TONY: "Protecting the homeland." Protecting your ass. Yeah, I'm going to hell. And for who? You?

GUSSIE: Yeah, great. Time to go, Tony.

(Gussie walks toward Tony. Tony shimmies out of the way and walks toward the griller.)

TONY: Make me.

(Tony pisses on the griller.)

My birthday gift. "Mi pissah es su pissah." *(Laughs)*

GUSSIE: Oh Jesus!

TONY: Hey, buy yourself a new one. It wasn't that much, right? Five grand? Spit.

(Terence takes a step toward Tony.)

TERENCE: OK, why don't you just get out of here?

(But Tony eludes Terence.)

TONY: This pool, what did it cost? Thirty grand? That table, what? A grand? That Mercedes out front . . .

GUSSIE: I don't have to justify myself to you.

TONY: But you do. You do. Those families I used to *visit*, they were real families. People who loved one another. I'm the only thing that stands between you and them. They'd be here right now eating your food if it weren't for me.

(Tony takes a step toward Gussie. Gussie laughs.)

GUSSIE: What are you going to do? Hit me? Kill me? This isn't some jungle, you drunken prick.

GRANMA BETTY: Gus, he's bigger than you.

TERENCE: Dad!

GUSSIE *(Turning to Michelle, like it's a joke)*: What's he going to do??? He's a fat old bag of wind.

TONY: C'mon, "Grampa," hit me. You know you want to.

(As Gussie turns to face Tony—SLAP—Tony strikes him in the face. Gussie's stunned, just stands there.)

Pussy. Your baby grandson is watching you. Show him what kind of man you are. Draft dodger. Bitch.

GUSSIE: I'm not going to hit you.

(SLAP. Tony strikes him again.)

OK . . . OK. Enough. You made your point.

TONY: Why don't you call your "armed response"?

(Gussie turns quickly, shoves at Tony, but misses. Tony yanks him with a quick judo move; Gussie finds himself on his hands and knees.)

GUSSIE: Michelle?!

JEREMY: Hit him, Grampa!

(Gussie stands back up.)

GRANMA BETTY: Gussie, just go in the house.

MICHELLE: Maybe you should, Gus. Go in.

TONY: Yeah, go in the house. Like your mommies tell you.

(Tony shoves him from behind. Gussie stumbles.)

TERENCE: OK, all right. Enough of this shit!

(Terence grabs Tony. In a flash, Tony chops him in the throat, punches him in the solar plexus; Terence is on his knees, gasping for breath.)

JEREMY: Daddy!

TONY: Climb *those* rocks, sonny boy.

(Tony stands over Terence, daring him to get up. Then he approaches Michelle and Roz. Gussie picks up Gloria's pepper grinder and comes up behind Tony.)

GRANMA BETTY: Gus!

TONY: Hey girls, how 'bout that, a Tony sandwich!

(Gussie viciously clobbers Tony from behind.)

MICHELLE: Gus!

(Tony turns but he's a split second too slow. BANG! Gussie slams Tony on the back of the head again. Granma Betty crosses herself.)

GRANMA BETTY: *Cristu!*

TONY *(Staggers)***:** Ohhh.

(As Tony turns to fight, Gussie hits him again, a homerun blow right upside his head.

Tony staggers toward the edge of the pool. He slips and falls in. Splash! Gussie, adrenalized, unbelieving, moves after him, ready to hit him one more time. Michelle embraces him, supportive.)

GUSSIE: MOTHERFUCKER!

DYLAN *(Watching Tony)***:** He's not moving, Dad. He's facedown!

MICHELLE: Gus, I think you knocked him out.

GRANMA BETTY: Attaboy, Gus.

GUSSIE: Go in the house. Gloria take her inside.

(Gloria is close to tears. Michelle, mesmerized, watches Tony floating in the pool.)

MICHELLE: Gus . . .

GLORIA: You really hurt him.

DYLAN: Dad, he's still not moving.

(Gussie looks over at Granma Betty, then at the pepper grinder.)

MICHELLE: Gussie, what are we going to do?

ROZ: We better do something.

(Gussie walks back to the cooler and grabs a beer. He finds a cigarette and lights it.)

GUSSIE *(Running through an alibi)*: He fell down. He'd been drinking. Lotta alcohol. He hit his head.

MICHELLE: Gus, shouldn't we get him out of the pool?

GUSSIE: *No!* We came back from the fireworks, he was in the pool. That's how we found him. That's all.

DYLAN: No bubbles. Definitely not breathing.

GUSSIE: Leave him there.

GRANMA BETTY: Good. He's the devil.

GUSSIE: No, he's not. He's not even my uncle.

(A distant rumbling—the sound of fireworks.)

JEREMY: The fireworks, the fireworks!!!!

(Gussie snaps into action.)

GUSSIE: OK, Jeremy, time to go to the fireworks.

JEREMY: With you, Grampa?

GUSSIE: Yeah!

ROZ *(Glancing at the pool)*: Michelle, except for this, today was lovely, thank you.

TERENCE: Dad, don't you think . . . ?

GUSSIE: What? Think what? Come on! Let's go. Roz, get in the Land Cruiser. There's enough room for all of us.

(Jeremy tugs at Gussie's hand.)

JEREMY: Come on, Grampa!

MICHELLE: I don't know if I feel like fireworks, Gus. And there's all this food.

GUSSIE: Just leave it. We'll clean it up later.

MICHELLE: Well, I'm parked behind you. So I better move my car. Do you have enough gas? No wait, I filled it when I went to the mall.

TERENCE: Wait a minute, I think I'm parked behind you . . .

GUSSIE: Don't worry about that.

ROZ: Do I need a jacket?

TERENCE: There's one in the Beemer.

GUSSIE: OK, so we're all set.

(Dylan goes. Jeremy pulls on Gussie, Terence starts to follow.)

GLORIA: What about me?

GUSSIE: Send us a postcard from Colorado.

GLORIA: Oh, so now I'm the bad guy?

MICHELLE: I should just put some tinfoil on the food.

GUSSIE: Forget the food! Let's go. *(To Gloria)* Gloria, you're giving me the load. I'm taking it.

(Gloria digests this.)

GLORIA: But I want to see the fireworks, too.

GUSSIE: So get in the car, what are you waiting for? The traffic is going to be nuts. Let's go, go, go!!!

(Gussie moves off with Terence and Jeremy as Michelle and Roz move out. Gloria follows. Granma Betty is left behind.)

GRANMA BETTY: We came to this country when I was very small. I can barely remember the old country. All I can know is that the rooms in our place were very small and it always smelled of cooking. My grandmother would cook all day. You could smell the cumin and the garlic all through the alley, everywhere. We were very poor. I owned one dress and I slept in the same bed as my sisters. So when there was a boat, we got on it and we left that stinking place. We would have done anything to get away, paid any price. And we came here, to America. *(She stops, as if finished, then)* You know what? That place is still over there, and it probably still smells of cooking. And sweat. And sewage. I could say I wish I was still there. But I'd be lying.

END OF PLAY

HUMPTY DUMPTY

I wanted to write a play for my brilliant wife and director, Jo Bonney.

Humpty Dumpty began as something to do with the millenium fears of total tech breakdown, what was known at the time as "Y2K." We workshopped it at the McCarter and by the spring of 2001 Emily Mann decided that the play would be part of the following year's schedule. In the fall, the attack on the World Trade Center occurred. Emily decided to press on with the play, now resonant with the fears we felt at that time. I made adjustments as best I could.

—**E.B.**

Production History

Humpty Dumpty received its world premiere at McCarter Theatre Center (Emily Mann, Artistic Director; Jeffrey Woodward, Managing Director) in Princeton, New Jersey, on March 26, 2002. It was directed by Jo Bonney; the set design was by Robert Brill, the costume design was by Ann Hould-Ward, the lighting design was by Ken Posner, the sound design was by John Gromada; the producing director was Mara Isaacs, the dramaturg was Janice Paran, the director of production was David York and the production stage manager was Cheryl Mintz. The cast was as follows:

NICOLE	Kathryn Meisle
MAX	Bruce Norris
TROY	Patrick Fabian
SPOON	Reiko Aylesworth
NAT	Michael Laurence

The Princeton workshop actors were Brienin Bryant, Evan Handler, Marcy Harriell, Jessica Hecht, Danny Hoch, Paul Marcarelli, Zak Orth, Martha Plimpton, Christopher Even Welch and C. J. Wilson.

Humpty Dumpty was subsequently produced at San Jose Repertory Theatre (Timothy Near, Artistic Director; Alexandra Urbanowski, Managing Director) in San Jose, California, on March 28, 2003. It was directed by John McCluggage; the set design was by Douglas Rogers, the costume design was by B. Modern, the lighting design was by Lap-Chi Chu, the sound design was by Steve Schoenbeck and the stage manager was Jenny Friend. The cast was as follows:

NICOLE	Elizabeth Hanly Rice
MAX	Saxon Palmer
TROY	Louis Lotorto
SPOON	Amy Brewczynski
NAT	Andy Murray

Characters

NICOLE, a book editor, thirties
MAX, her husband, a novelist, thirties
TROY, Nicole and Max's friend, a screenwriter, thirties
SPOON, his girlfriend, an actress, thirties
NAT, the caretaker, fifties

Setting

A vacation home in upstate New York. The present.

ACT ONE

Scene 1

Late afternoon light pours into a roomy vacation home that had once been a barn. The spacious room is furnished with collectible pottery, bookcases and kilim throw rugs. Comfy armchairs, a couch and an oak table face an enormous bluestone fireplace. Elevated about two feet above the space is the kitchen. Behind it, a windowpaned door leads to a glass "mudroom," porch and the outdoors. An upstage balcony leads to three bedrooms.

Nicole enters from outside wrestling luggage and groceries. She is on her cell phone. Her tone is clipped and brash.

NICOLE *(To phone)*: Right. Uh-huh. No, business-class is fine, I don't need first. But get me priority check-in no matter what. And did you give them the frequent-flyer number? Oh shit, you're breaking up . . . damn!

(Nicole puts down the groceries and luggage and finds a good signal for her cell phone. Max arrives with a box of books.)

No there, OK. You ordered the special meal? What? No. That's *not* the same. No, cheese is *not* the same as tofu, Sara. Tell them it has to be *totally* nondairy. And make sure they have bottled water. If not . . . Hold on Sara. *(To Max)* What?

MAX: Did you take my laptop out of the car?

I can't find my laptop.

It's on your shoulder.
(To phone) We just got here. Literally just walked in. It's nice. It's . . .

(Sees it) Oh, right.

(Max drops the box of books and heads back out for luggage. Nicole wanders.)

. . . a little weird. But I guess all new places are weird. That's the definition of weird, isn't it? So, Sara? Call the car company, put the confirmation number on my voice-mail, and maybe I'll talk to you tomorrow. Hello? What? OK. Bye. *(Ends call)*

(Max returns with luggage. He's so overwhelmed with stuff, he hasn't even looked around the place.)

MAX: I think I got everything. Fuck.

(Max drops onto the couch, exhausted. Nicole flops down next to him. Suddenly stillness fills the air. A chickadee chirps.)

NICOLE: Here we are! A mere five and a half hours later.

MAX: I need drugs.

NICOLE: This *is* drugs. Just more expensive.

(Restless, Max jumps up to inventory what they've got.)

MAX: So . . . Cable with HBO. *(Runs upstairs, pokes head in bedrooms; from off)* Three working fireplaces. Views. Lots of views. Cedar Jacuzzi for two. *(Hops down into kitchen)* And let's not forget the fully equipped chef's kitchen. *(Checking)* Stove doesn't light. *(Looking through the glass mudroom)* Not to mention nearby walking paths and pastoral pond with gazebo. All in a life-affirming, isolated, picturesque setting far from the madding crowd.

(Max opens cabinets and closets. Nicole wanders upstairs to explore the bedrooms.)

NICOLE *(Off)*: Lots of quilts and handmade pottery. Macramé wall-hangings. Fireplaces in each bedroom. Cedar Jacuzzi.

MAX: I said that already. I said cedar Jacuzzi.

NICOLE *(Off)*: No cable up here. And no fax machine anywhere. Cell phone barely works. And how do we do email?

MAX: We don't. That's the point. For one week, we don't do anything. No faxes. No email.

NICOLE *(Returning)*: How much did all this rustic splendor cost? *(Eyeing kitchen appliances)* Espresso machine.

MAX: Three grand. Plus complimentary ski-lift tickets.

NICOLE: It's too early for snow, isn't it?

MAX: That's why they're complimentary.

(Nicole hugs Max, kisses him, then moves off again.)

NICOLE: You did good. I prefer Saint Bart's, but like you said, this way we avoid airports, lines, X-ray machines. No delays, no terrorists. Just downtime. Good old-fashioned downtime.

MAX: Plus the Caribbean is so, you know, *nineties*. Monotonous white beaches, everything stinking of sunblock. Third-world service personnel grinning and shuffling, trying to guilt you out for being American. You have to stay drunk and play golf and tennis all day long just to stave off the boredom. I *hate* golf and tennis.

NICOLE: You left out snorkeling in the blue-green water.

MAX: Fuck the blue-green water! The whole thing smacks of decadence and colonialism. This is much better, healthier—more patriotic even. We'll go for hikes. We'll rock-climb. We'll contemplate nature. We'll breathe pure oxygen.

NICOLE: *Cold* pure oxygen. Where's the thermostat?

MAX: No, wait, lemme make a fire. If we're going to do this, let's do it right.

(Nicole searches shelves as Max works at the fireplace.)

NICOLE: Jigsaw puzzles. Scrabble. Hmmmm. *Art and Antiques, House and Garden, American Quilting!* Oh my—*The Joy of Sex!*

MAX: There you go! See? We'll try out new erotic positions on a bearskin rug! *(Finds a note on the mantel)* A note!

(Nicole finds a record player and a box of records. Max reads the note out loud:)

"Trash day is Tuesday. Be sure to fasten the lids tightly or the raccoons *will* get in. Keep thermostat on sixty-eight. Don't flush tampons or other foreign objects down the toilet." Foreign objects?! "Feel free to use the homemade peanut butter." *What*?!!! "Emergency numbers . . ." Yada yada. "Extra quilts in the cupboard." This place is the quilt mecca. Oh, and this is in bold: "There's no smoking of any kind." And I just bought that new crack pipe! "Have a great time! Ted and Sondra!" Well, they sound like loads of fun.

(Max lights some paper under the wood in the fireplace.)

NICOLE: Check out this vinyl! Jethro Tull. Joan Baez. Van Morrison. I bet they went to Woodstock.

(Nicole puts a record on: Van Morrison's Moondance. *Max steps back, the fireplace comes to life.)*

MAX: Voilà!

(Nicole wraps her arms around Max.)

NICOLE: You did that so well! A regular frontiersman. I'm impressed. My own Daniel Boone.

(Entwined, Nicole and Max watch the fire.)

How 'bout this? Since I am ovulating right this very second, why don't we put all these quilts and sex books to work and get me pregnant!

MAX: Troy and Spoon are going to be here any minute.

NICOLE: We'll have a quickie: "Wham, bam, thank you, ma'am."

MAX: I'm not that kind of guy.

NICOLE: Every guy is that kind of guy. *(Rubs his shoulders)* You're very tense. You need to relax.

MAX: I'm relaxed.

NICOLE: No you're not.

MAX: I'm in the country, aren't I? I mean, how much more relaxed can I get? Maybe I should go out and chop down a tree?

NICOLE *(Nuzzling him)*: C'mon, let's fuck.

MAX: Nicole, you're undercutting my need to obsess.

NICOLE *(More nuzzling)*: What are you obsessed about?

MAX: Everything. Money, my novel, selling the book, selling out, money. Pretty much money.

NICOLE: Don't you want to get me pregnant?

MAX: Of course I do.

(They start kissing. Nicole takes Max's hand.)

NICOLE: Time to pack all that anxiety away. Time to become obsessed with *me*. Who knows? We might relax and start enjoying ourselves. Come on Davy Crockett, you can make another fire upstairs.

MAX: I thought I was Daniel Boone.

(They begin to move up the steps. Kisses. Hands all over each other. They laugh like kids. Max strips her clothes off. They're at the top of the steps. They enter the bedroom. Long pause. The phone rings. Nicole quickly reemerges in a teddy and sexy stockings. To Max, over her shoulder:)

NICOLE: I just want to see who it is.

MAX *(Off)*: Nicole!

NICOLE: Only take a sec.

MAX *(Off)*: Who'd you give this number to?

NICOLE: No one. Well, Billy, but that's because . . .

(The answering machine kicks in.)

ANSWERING MACHINE *(Woman's voice)*: Hello, this is Ted and Sondra. *(Guy's voice)* Hi! *(Woman's voice)* We're not here right now, so leave a message. If not, have a great 24/7! *(Beep)*

BILLY'S VOICE: Nicole? It's Billy. We have a little problem . . .

NICOLE *(To Max)*: We were on deadline and . . .

BILLY: The author wants a note re: the typeface and we didn't figure that into the page count, so the books won't break out evenly. He's really adamant about it. In fact, now he says he wants the acknowledgments . . .

MAX: You gave your copy editor this number?

NICOLE: I had to.

MAX: Well, call him back later.

NICOLE *(Moving downstairs toward the phone)*: I can't, it has to be done by Monday. *(Picks up the phone)* Hey. It's me. No, nothing, Billy, just hanging out. What's up? Uh-huh.

(Max joins her. Thinking it won't be a long call, he caresses her as she listens to Billy. Nicole waves Max away. He stands a few feet off, waiting.)

Uh-huh. Uh-huh. OK. OK. OK. No. Just a sec Billy. *(To Max)* Go make your fire! I'll be right up.

(Max makes a sign to hurry up and goes up the stairs to the bedroom.)

Yeah. Well, listen, Billy, that's the way it is. He just has to deal with it. No. I can't call him now. I can't. Just do it, I don't care. So OK. OK? Huh? Sara? I guess, put her on.

(Nicole looks up and sees that Max is gone. She starts rolling down her stockings.)

What? No, I can't take a *cab*! What happened to the car service? *(Beat)* Oh, fuck them. I always have a car when I get to O'Hare, and that's it. Just make it happen.

(A man, Nat, can be seen entering the mudroom with a toolbox. He observes Nicole for a moment before rapping on the glass.)

Just a sec, Sara. *(Startled)* Hello?

(Nicole grabs Max's jacket, which is lying nearby, and slips it on.)

NAT *(From the mudroom)*: I work for the Murphys . . .
NICOLE: Who?
NAT: The Murphys? Ted and Sondra?

NICOLE: Oh. Right. *(Calling out)* Max?!

NAT: Mind if I . . . ?

NICOLE *(Standing)*: No, no, come on in. Max?

NAT *(Entering)*: I'm sorry. I, uh, I just wanted to say hello. My name's Nat. I look after the house. You're the guests?

NICOLE: Yes. Right. Nat. Nice to meet you. I'm Nicole.

(Max, in his boxers, appears at the bedroom door, pulling on a shirt.)

MAX: Is that them?

NICOLE: No, it's *Nat*. Works for the Murphys. *(To phone)* Oh, Sara? Just a sec.

MAX: Who are "the Murphys"?

NICOLE *(To Max)*: The people we rented the house from?

MAX: Oh right.

(Max disappears into the bedroom. Nicole holds a "one-sec" finger up to Nat.)

NICOLE *(To phone)*: OK, so. Do that. And see if you can upgrade to a suite. And don't forget I have to be at least three rooms away from the ice machine.

(Max reappears fully dressed and trots down the stairs, seeing Nat for the first time.)

(To phone) Just tell them, Sara. They'll figure it out.

NAT *(To Max)*: Ted said I should look at the stove.

MAX: Oh, right.

(Nat steps over to the stove and flicks on one of the burners. Max gives a panicky look to Nicole as Nat gets engrossed in the stove.)

NICOLE *(To Max)*: I'm going upstairs. Hang it up for me?

(*Nicole moves upstairs into the bedroom.*)

MAX (*To Nat*): You know, it's no big deal, why don't you just leave it?
NAT: Oh, no, no. If your stove doesn't work, how you gonna eat?
NICOLE (*Off, shouting*): OK!

(*Max hangs up the phone. Nat tinkers with the stove.*)

MAX: It won't light. But I can use matches.
NAT: Not a problem at all. Just needs an adjustment.

(*Beat. Max watches Nat.*)

MAX: So. Think we'll get snow?
NAT: Sooner or later.
MAX: I better check *The Old Farmer's Almanac*, eh?

(*Nat contorts himself over the top of the stove.*)

NAT: Or The Weather Channel. Say, hand me that socket wrench there? (*Points to his toolbox*)
MAX: Sure thing. This one? (*Hands him a wrench*)
NAT: The *socket* wrench. There.
MAX: Oh, right. (*Hands it to him*)
NAT: Thanks.

(*Max impotently watches Nat work. Nicole comes out to the landing and looks down.*)

NICOLE: Max?

(*Max looks up to Nicole, shrugs, gives her the one-sec sign. Nicole goes back into the bedroom.*)

MAX: Uh, so where do we go around here for groceries?

NAT: Well, you got milk, bread, soda, Lotto tickets, down at the gas station on Mason Hill Road. Need anything fancy, you gotta go down the turnpike a way, where the Wal-Mart is.

MAX: That's a trip. Must be twenty miles.

NAT: Uh-huh.

(Nat drops the stove top on his finger.)

Owww! Cheese Louise!

(Troy and Spoon, lugging travel bags and groceries, appear in the mudroom. Troy is dressed in Dolce & Gabbana, Spoon is in Prada "country attire." Max rushes to the backdoor, opens it. Spoon and Troy enter.)

TROY *(On his cell phone):* . . . his notes were OK. Predictable, but OK. He wants a female angle so I'll lay in a love interest . . .

MAX *(Shouting):* Nicole! They're here!

TROY: . . . ramp up the confrontation with his dad before act three, and he'll buy it.

(Max hugs Spoon. Troy finishes his call.)

MAX: You're here! Didn't expect you so early! Hi!

SPOON: You told Troy five hours, so he had to make it in four. Did ninety all the way.

TROY *(Into cell phone):* Look, I'm here. I should jump. But tell him the three thousand as production bonus is a deal-breaker. Just do it, Keith. *(Ends call; turning to Max)* Maximilian! *(Hugs Max)* Hey man! Look at you!

(Max and Troy hug. Nicole emerges from the bedroom, fully dressed. Spoon takes in the place.)

SPOON: This place is amazing! What is it? A barn?

MAX: I guess so, yeah. A new-age barn.

SPOON: I *love* this! *(Looking around)* It's like we're in the middle of nowhere! Troy, this is like Bobby's place in Montana.

MAX: Thirty-five acres surrounded by a thousand square miles of state forest. This area hasn't changed since the eighteenth century. *(Shouts)* Nicole?!

TROY: Bobby has over three hundred acres.

NICOLE: Troy! Hi! Hi! Spoon! Max, help them with their stuff!

NAT: Lemme give you a hand there.

(Troy, Max and Nat go out as Nicole comes downstairs.)

SPOON: Hi, Nicole!

NICOLE: You made it!

SPOON: Barely! Delayed in L.A., delayed in New York. I thought we'd never land.

(Troy and Max return hauling boxes and bags.)

TROY: They wanted to strip-search Spoon. Full body-cavity inspection. I had to threaten them with a pair of fingernail clippers.

SPOON: Stop it! They made me take off my shoes! I mean, duh, like I'm going to blow up the plane with my shoes, right.

NICOLE *(To Troy, a double kiss)*: Hi. Hi. All this food! Did you happen to bring any soy milk, Troy?

TROY: Soy milk, no. *But* I did discover a mind-blowing Australian shiraz and two Napa pinot grigios that are indistinguishable from mother's milk. And check this out, '92 Haut-Brion—$250 a bottle.

(Troy turns to Nat, who is hauling in a cooler.)

How you doin'? I'm Troy, by the way. This is Spoon.

NAT: Hi. Uh . . . "Spoon"?

SPOON: Spoon. As in tea*spoon*, table*spoon*. Cutlery. My parents were hippies. It's short for spoonful.

NAT: OK.

(Spoon grows shy before Nat's gaze. She turns to Troy.)

SPOON: My hair's weird. Is my hair weird?

MAX: Nat's here doing some work.

SPOON: Wow, cool! You're a writer, too?

NAT: No. No. Just, you know, fixing the stove.

SPOON: Really? I've always wanted to be able to do that, you know, fix things.

(Max is into the groceries; Nat returns to the stove.)

MAX: Edamame, good. Belgian butter. And we got the jumbo shrimp.

SPOON: Not farm shrimp, Max! I can't eat anything raised on antibiotics or hormones.

(Spoon zips up the steps. Max calls up after her:)

MAX: No, no. I think they're just big due to Darwinian selection. Survival-of-the-fittest shrimp.

TROY: Check out this off-the-hook focaccia! Ninety-year-old Italian lady on Elizabeth Street bakes it in an authentic stone oven her father built in 1910. *(Opens a container of olives)*

(Spoon calls out from the top of the stairs.)

SPOON: Troy! This sunset, wow! The view is amazing!

TROY *(Chewing)***:** Nicole, come here!

NICOLE: What?

TROY: Open your mouth.

NICOLE: No.

(Nicole opens her mouth. Troy feeds her an olive. Spoon disappears into the bedroom.)

TROY: These are the olives the Greek gods ate on Mount Olympus. Ambrosial. Single estate. The bomb.

NICOLE: Mmmmmm. Max, did you remember to get the little grape tomatoes?

MAX: I got the vine-ripened Dutch ones instead. Troy, when did you start talking this hip-hop lingo? You sound like P. Diddy on a bad day.

TROY: It's from hanging with studio executives. They feel better about paying me my quote when they're not quite sure what I'm saying. *(More food)* Dig this cheese! Aged sheep's milk from, get this, *Kosovo*! How cool is that? And Armenian string cheese, the real stuff, not that shrink-wrapped supermarket dreck. Max, Max, Max—check out this caviar.

MAX: Caviar isn't yellow.

TROY: Oh yes it *is*! This, my friend, is *sterlet*. Formerly reserved for the Shah of Iran.

NICOLE: Caviar?

TROY *(To Nat)*: Can't sip the Stoli without the fish eggs!

(Spoon is sailing in and out of the bedrooms.)

SPOON: Fireplaces! And quilts! It's so nurturing!

NICOLE: Troy, we're only here for the week.

TROY: That's what they said in Stalingrad!

MAX: This is known as conspicuous consumption.

TROY: Wrong! It takes discrimination, sophistication and skill to assemble this pile of goodies. It may be conspicuous, but it is not obvious.

MAX: Yellow caviar.

TROY: Listen, when you're gazing out at the purple mountains, imbibing the most impeccable armagnac, nibbling the silkiest brie on a slice of sun-ripened Normandy pear, when you are enjoying a singular and perfect moment in your life, you will thank me.

(Spoon comes back down. She goes to a window.)

NAT: Your stove's all set.

SPOON: Oh, Troy, check out the deer, she's so cute! Just nibbling the bushes. Troy, look!

NAT: Oh you'll see everything up here: deer, coyote, wild turkey.

SPOON: That's so great!

NAT: S'posed to be mountain lion up on the ridge.

NICOLE: Aren't they extinct?

NAT: Might be, but something ate my dog and it wasn't a raccoon.

MAX *(Moving to Nat)*: Thanks a lot, man. *(Reaching into his pocket)* What do I . . . ?

NAT: Oh, no, no. No charge! Listen, that's my number over on the fireplace. Just gimme a ring you guys need anything.

MAX: Well, uh . . . nice meeting you, Nat.

(Spoon beams at Nat as he leaves.)

TROY: Wow. Right out of a Norman Rockwell painting.

SPOON: What a nice man!

MAX: Guess he keeps an eye on the place. Plows the drive, rakes the leaves, like that.

TROY: Wrestles mountain lions.

NICOLE: No wonder he's in such good shape.

MAX: He's authentic, that's all. Not full of attitude like us urban types. Just does his thing.

SPOON: It's kind of Zen-like.

TROY: "Authentic"? How?

MAX: Real. Genuine.

TROY: How is that guy more genuine than you or me?

MAX: You know what I'm saying. He doesn't seek validation from abstract achievement—money, kudos, a place in the pecking order. There is no pecking order in his life, there's no hierarchy out here. He just deals with the bare necessities. Eats, works, sleeps. Lives.

NICOLE: You don't know that.

MAX: Come on. Look at him. He's a totally centered human being. Somebody who knows who he is. Unpretentious. Clear minded.

SPOON: I see it. He's off the grid in every way.

NICOLE: That is a large pot of simmering crap.

MAX: Hey, all I know is I'd love to have that guy's life! Keeping it simple. No mental static. No bullshit.

SPOON: I am so with you, Max.

TROY: No, you know what? You're right. It must be *so* rewarding. Driving an old truck. Making a big five bucks an hour. Doing yardwork for a living. Being illiterate. Having sex with the sheep. Ba-a-a-a-ah!

SPOON *(Laughing)***:** Troy! You so suck!

MAX: Troy, you know what your problem is? You are totally parochial. You think the world begins at Morton's and ends at The Penisula Club.

TROY: Doesn't it? So . . . listen we have to make a big decision: shiraz or champagne?

(Spoon's cell phone rings.)

SPOON *(Into phone)***:** Hello? Brian! Hi, honey. Great. Huh? Where? L.A.? But I just got here!

(Nicole's cell phone rings.)

NICOLE *(Into phone)***:** Yeah? Uh-huh. What are you telling me, Billy?

(Troy's cell phone rings. He answers it. The three talk on their phones for some time, adjusting positions for better reception.)

SPOON: Well, because I'm on *vacation!* Oh, I can barely hear you!

TROY: Yo! Dog! Hey!! Good. Good. Kicking back. Hanging with my homies. S'up? Uh-huh . . . *(Jots on his Palm Pilot)*

NICOLE: But, Billy, why can't you handle this?

SPOON: Can't I do it another time?

TROY: Keith, Keith, Keith, it's all solvable. No. Wait. Listen . . . hello?

NICOLE: No, why do I have to talk to his agent? We have nothing to talk about.

SPOON: I want to do it. I do. But . . . are you mad at me? Don't be mad at me.

NICOLE: Billy, I can't believe this hasn't been taken care of. NO. Do *not* give him this number.

TROY: Give him my number, I'll talk to him.

SPOON: Give me their number, I'll make it better.

NICOLE: Of course I'm pissed off. *Jesus*, Billy!

TROY: All right, listen. I'll tell him I've always wanted to work with him, he's a great artist, I wrote the role for him, blah-blah, woof-woof. OK? Keith, you worry too much.

NICOLE: *Billy*, the deadline has passed.

SPOON: I'm sorry. I'm a fuck-up. I know. But I really can't. Tell them I'm sick. But I'd love to come on the show like maybe next month? OK? Is that going to be OK?

(Max's cell phone is silent. He checks it—nothing.)

TROY: Keith, leave it to me. Just leave it. OK?

SPOON: Thank you. I love you, too. I know you're only thinking of me. OK? OK.

NICOLE: Are you sure? No, don't tell me you're sure if you're not sure. OK. No. I said OK. Gotta go. *(Ends call)*

SPOON: Gotta go. *(Ends call)*

TROY: Gotta go. *(Ends call)*

NICOLE: Fuck. If I'm not there, there's a total meltdown.

SPOON: My manager's pissed off at me.

MAX: Is that the thing you're doing at Paramount??

TROY: Nah, turned that in last week. That was the people at Interforce? They're producing my spec script. They go weak at the knees when they get on the phone with a star.

MAX: But I thought your spec was with Pressman?

NICOLE: You're writing *two* screenplays at the same time?

TROY: Three if you include the HBO thing, four if you include the production polish for Warner's. I'm like the guy with the spinning plates. Spin, spin, spin.

SPOON *(Looks out the window)*: Oh look, now there's a little rabbit! She *sees* us! She does! I wonder what she's thinking?

(Troy nuzzles Spoon from behind. He kisses her neck.)

TROY: She's thinking, I'm horny—where's Bugs?

SPOON *(Coy)*: Yeah?

(Troy begins to kiss and fondle Spoon right in front of Nicole and Max. Max and Nicole ignore them. After a moment, Troy and Spoon "come out of it," obviously hungry for more . . .)

TROY: You know what guys? We're going to take our stuff up and unpack.

(Troy and Spoon grab some luggage and skedaddle to their room. Door slam. Giggling is heard from behind the door.)

MAX: Do you, uh, want to "unpack," too?

NICOLE: What?

MAX: Do you want to . . . you know, go upstairs?

NICOLE: Uh . . . maybe after dinner. You know? I don't think I can . . . when they're . . .

MAX: Right . . .

NICOLE: . . . in the next room . . .

MAX: Right.

(Beat.)

NICOLE: I should call Billy back. He's in way over his depth.

MAX: Yeah.

NICOLE: Or not.

MAX: Whatever.

NICOLE: Let me just call him and then we'll unpack.

MAX: Good. *(Pause)* I didn't realize Troy was doing so well.

(Nicole dials her cell phone. Max watches the rabbit out the window.)

I know what the rabbit is thinking.

NICOLE *(Not really listening)*: What?

MAX: Why isn't my cell phone ringing?

Scene 2

Night. Living room. Troy, Nicole and Spoon sit by the fire playing Scrabble. The TV is on but muted. Max is in the kitchen, preparing desserts; the remains of dinner lie scattered. Bob Dylan plays on the stereo.

MAX: It's all a function of American hegemony. I mean, the fucking IMF doesn't give a shit. They're happy to see the third world go down the tubes as long as we preserve the good life back home in the empire. Troy, did you see that picture last week in the *Times*? Little boy in the middle of a garbage dump outside Rio? Pathetic. Makes a living picking drinking straws out of the garbage.

NICOLE: *I* saw it. It made me nauseous!

MAX: Spoon, would you like the hazelnut torte or bittersweet chocolate mousse with raspberries?

SPOON: A little of both. What does he do with the drinking straws?

MAX: Oh the kid? Washes them out and sells them to restaurants. Ten for a penny.

NICOLE: Probably why we got the raging shits in Tulum last year.

TROY: You should have told me you were in Tulum! I know the best little café, right on the beach. Just a shack, your toes are in sand while you eat.

SPOON: We're going to Puerto Vallarta in January.

TROY: You guys should come with us. Do a little fishing, a little peyote, eat the worm in the bottle.

MAX: I can't believe you're on a vacation talking about your *next* vacation!

TROY: It's true. Sad but true. Nicole, are you digging this wine? Earthy, with just the barest hint of a blackberry finish. '82 bordeaux, you can't beat it. Two glasses and it's like a week in Provence.

(Max joins the group with the desserts.)

MAX: Actually it would be like a week in Bordeaux. Provence is a *region*, Bordeaux is a *city*. They're both in France, that's about all they have in common.

SPOON: Max, you know everything. Is Xanadu a word?

(Nicole pours herself another glass of wine.)

NICOLE: "In Xanadu did Kublai Khan a stately pleasure-dome decree . . ." etcetera, etcetera. The actual Xanadu was the summer palace of the Mongol royalty at Shangtu. And I think maybe Omar Khayyám had something to do with it.

MAX: Omar Khayyám wrote the *Rubáiyát*, Edward FitzGerald translated it. Coleridge wrote *Xanadu*. It's possible Fitz-Gerald and Coleridge knew each other. Same era, different generations.

SPOON: Oh. So I can use it?

TROY: It's not your turn. It's *my* turn.

SPOON: Troy! Be gentle, I've never done this before!

(Troy kisses her. They get into it. Nicole sips her wine.)

NICOLE: Troy, this wine *is* nice.

TROY: Thank you, Spoon refuses to try it.

SPOON: That's not true! I'm just taking a little break from alcohol. Trying to realign, you know? Only spring water, tea and organic berry juice.

TROY: Spoon's concluded she's an alcoholic.

SPOON: I have done no such thing. I'm just not drinking.

TROY: Because you're afraid of losing control.

SPOON: I feel better this way. Serene.

TROY: Spoon believes in a perfect world where everyone meditates every day and eats no meat and where no animals are harmed . . . ever. *(Laying Scrabble tiles)*

SPOON: I would love that world.

TROY: I'd be bored shitless in three days. *Fur-bish.*

MAX: "Furbish." There's no such word! *Furbish?*

TROY: Of course there is. You *re-furbish* something, so you must be able to *furbish* it. Four, six, double word on the I—thirty.

(Spoon picks up the dictionary.)

SPOON: "Furbish: To brighten by cleaning or rubbing. To restore to attractive or serviceable condition. Renovate." You win, Troy. *(She kisses him)*

TROY: Max, you may know everything, but I know more words. And have tighter abs.

SPOON *(Moving tiles)*: "Xanadu." Fifteen. Oh! And I have a double word! Thirty!

MAX *(Sulking)*: D-U. Not D-O-O.

NICOLE: Max. Relax, Max.

MAX *(Huffy)*: "Wisdom." Fourteen. Double word. Twenty-eight. *(Moves tiles)* We'll see who knows more words. You are all doomed. I am the Tiger Woods of Scrabble.

NICOLE: I met Tiger Woods last week. Nice guy. Sexy. *(Addressing her tiles)* L-E-M-M-I-N-G: "lemming." Double letter on the M, and triple word—thirty-nine.

TROY (*Makes a cursory glance at his tiles and quickly throws some down*): Z-A-R-F: "zarf." A holder, usually of ornamental metal for a coffee cup. Double letter on the Z. Twenty-six. Hey, did you see Kurt's new novel already sold for a nice fat two mil?

NICOLE: Two point five. Binky cut the deal.

MAX: Well his last book was shit. "Zarf," huh?

TROY: Hey, I *like* Kurt's books. They're trashy and smart.

(*Max gets up to find another bottle of wine.*)

MAX: Boutique intellectualism for the masses.

NICOLE: "The masses"?

MAX: The masses, the general public. All those average citizens who don't live in New York or L.A., and who read *People* magazine and watch the Oscars.

NICOLE: We read *People* magazine and watch the Oscars.

MAX: Yes, yes. But we do it *ironically*.

TROY: Well, it got him the Pulitzer.

MAX: So what?

TROY: Jealous?

MAX: I can't be jealous of an empty facade.

SPOON: Is it Puh-litzer or Pew-litzer?

TROY: I thought it's Pooh-litzer.

SPOON: Max, I read your story in the *New Yorker*. I loved how you described that old man's thoughts. Like you were *so* inside his head! How do you do that?

MAX: Most people have an inner child. I have an inner geriatric.

SPOON: It was wonderful. I can't wait to read the whole book.

MAX: Thank you.

TROY: You should adapt it as a film!

NICOLE: He's going to. Max, didn't you tell Troy about the deal?

MAX: No, I . . .

NICOLE: Max just sold the option!

TROY: And you didn't tell me! Your best friend? When?

MAX: Two weeks ago. They took me out to lunch and they say they're going to buy it.

TROY: Lunch? Where? Bouley? Jean Georges? Nobu?

MAX: I don't know, Troy! Someplace uptown. I wasn't paying any attention.

TROY: They're buying the book or just the option? And you're doing the screenplay? What are we talking about here? Six figures? Seven?

MAX: I let the agents deal with all that.

TROY: Oh, we're being humble. Very endearing.

MAX: It's not about the money.

TROY: Of course it's not about the money. What is it about then? The art? C'mon, Max! You're dancing with the devil, you might as well enjoy yourself. Don't deny yourself the pleasure of gloating, you've been busting your ass for too long. *(Lifting his glass)* A toast to Maxie (to paraphrase Oscar Wilde): "When I was young, I thought fame and fortune was everything. Now that I'm old, I *know* it is."

SPOON: Cheers!

ALL: Cheers!

(Nicole changes the music: the Rolling Stones' "Brown Sugar." She dances to it. Troy gets up and dances with her.)

MAX: Spoon, what are *you* working on?

SPOON: Oh I might do this movie about Søren Kierkegaard? The existential philosopher? Very dark. According to the script he was really hung up on a girl named Regina. That's me.

MAX: A film about Søren Kierkegaard? Who's directing?

(Spoon gets up and starts dancing with Nicole and Troy.)

SPOON: Spielberg. They're shooting in Copenhagen and everything.

MAX: Really? *(Miffed but not sure why)* Spoon, it's your turn.

NICOLE: Max, come dance with me!

MAX: I thought we were playing . . . Spoon, it's your turn.

NICOLE: Max! . . .

> (*Troy floats by the table, grabs his wine, returns to the women, putting his arms around both of them. They love his playful energy.*)

TROY: Say, why don't we have an orgy this weekend? Throw the car keys in a bowl?

> (*Nicole comes over to Max and leans over him.*)

NICOLE: I have a great word: J-I-G-G-Y.

MAX: That's not a word.

NICOLE: Sure it is. As in "jiggy-jiggy."

> (*Troy is dancing close to Spoon. They fall onto the couch and are smooching.*)

MAX: Anyway, it's not your turn. It's Spoon's turn. Spoon, come back to the table.

NICOLE: I'll take her turn.

MAX: You can't do that!

> (*Nicole and Max struggle slightly and she jogs the table.*)

Now it's all fucked-up! It's ruined!

> (*Nicole plops down into Max's lap. Giddy.*)

NICOLE: Hi.

MAX: I was winning! I had a great word.

NICOLE: I *know* you did, baby.

> (*THE LIGHTS GO OUT. The TV set blinks off, music cuts.*)

MAX: What the . . .

NICOLE: Max?

MAX: We must have too many things going at the same time and blew a fuse. Wait a sec, I saw a flashlight by the fridge.

(Max stumbles up into the kitchen. Sound of him hitting furniture.)

Shit!

NICOLE: You OK?

MAX: Fine. Wait. Don't anybody move!

TROY: You need help?

MAX: No. Wait. Wait. Here. Owww.

NICOLE: Max! Are you OK?

(Max finds the flashlight and snaps it on.)

MAX: I think I saw a fuse box downstairs.

(Max exits to the basement to fix the fuse.)

TROY: How much are we paying for this dump anyway?

MAX *(Off)*: DID THAT DO ANYTHING?

NICOLE: NO! WHERE ARE YOU?

MAX *(Off)*: I DON'T THINK IT'S THE FUSE!

(Troy and Spoon grope each other in the dark.)

SPOON: Actually this isn't so bad. Take your time.

(Max enters, wiping cobwebs out of his hair.)

MAX: I'm pretty sure it's not the fuse. They must have candles and matches somewhere. Hold this.

(Nicole holds the flashlight. Max rummages through drawers.)

NICOLE: Let's call that Nat guy.

MAX: What's his number? Uh, Nicole, read the number off that note on the mantel.

(Nicole uses the flashlight to make her way to the fireplace. Max picks up the phone.)

SPOON: I'll find some candles.

MAX: On the fridge I think.

NICOLE: 2-5-5-7-3 . . .

MAX: Wait.

(Spoon lights candles.)

TROY *(Singing)*: "Strangers in the night . . ."

MAX: Shut up, Troy. Something's wrong with the phone.

NICOLE: What?

MAX: Fast busy signal.

SPOON: Probably everybody's using their phone. Overload.

NICOLE: You think?

MAX: Try your cell, Spoon.

NICOLE: I don't like this, Max! What if it's a terrorist attack or something?

TROY: Nicole, it's a fuse.

NICOLE: It's not a fuse. Max just checked the fuse.

TROY: Well, it's something. But it's not a terrorist attack. Terrorists don't attack renovated barns.

MAX: It's cool. It's cool.

SPOON: Oh, shit, my cell phone just went dead. Troy, where's the charger?

TROY: Where you going to plug it in?

SPOON: Oh. Right.

TROY: Here, I got mine. What's the number?

NICOLE: Well, it says 2-5-5-7-3-1 . . . but you need the area code. What's the area code up here?

MAX: Uh . . . shit. I have the real estate agent's number in my wallet.

NICOLE: Look on the phone. The phone, the house phone.

MAX: Oh, right.

(Max takes a candle and tries to inspect the phone.)

It's either 518 or 618, I can't make it out.

TROY: Max. Don't bother. My cell won't lock on. Just keeps searching.

(Headlights can be seen outside. A powerful light waves through the gloom in the mudroom.)

NICOLE: Oh wow. Max! This is freaky.

NAT: Hello?

(Nat enters. His Coleman lamp illuminates the room.)

MAX: Yes! Hi! Nat? Great!

NAT: Electric's out.

TROY: Is *that* why it's so dark in here!

MAX: At first I thought it was a breaker or a fuse . . .

NICOLE: Is it something serious?

NAT: Nah. Probably some knucklehead hit a telephone pole. Take 'em couple of hours to fix it. Happens all the time.

(Nat goes to the sink and begins to fill some pans and large bowls with water.)

MAX: A telephone pole?

NAT: Sorry 'bout that. Just the way it is up here.

NICOLE: And they can fix it in, what did you say, two hours?

NAT: Usually that's what it takes. Might take all night. Really dunno at this point. Look, you got candles and I'll leave this lamp here. The water pump runs on electric, this is just the water left in the pipes. Should hold you for the night. Just don't flush. And the oil burner needs a spark, so you might want to put some big logs in the fire before you go to bed. But hey, you're on vacation, right? Kick back, enjoy the quiet. I'll be by in the morning, check in on you. OK? Just watch out for the mountain lions. They're hungry this time of year. Just jokin'. *(Laughs)* All right then. 'Night all.

(Nat leaves.)

TROY: Well there you go. The terrorists drove all the way up here and ran into a telephone pole.

SPOON: Leave it alone, Troy.

NICOLE *(Pensive)*: So.

SPOON: So here we are. No lights. But that's not so bad.

TROY: And we can't flush.

SPOON: We *can*. We just, you know, shouldn't.

NICOLE: Max?

MAX: Here we are! It's like a camping trip.

TROY: Should we crack out the marshmallows and sing songs around the fire?

NICOLE: I'm going to bed.

(Nicole heads upstairs.)

MAX: Nicole? Are you OK?

NICOLE: Yeah. Just . . . you know, tired.

MAX: OK. I'll be up in a sec.

TROY: You know what? I'm going to crash, too.

MAX: Well, if everybody . . .

SPOON: Look how pretty the fire is.

MAX: Yeah. It is. It's primal isn't it?

(Troy makes his way upstairs.)

TROY: G'night.

MAX: 'Night.

SPOON: The flames never stop changing. A million shapes and colors. And it's all the energy of the tree's life, all those years of living, just exploding outward into the air. Maybe that's what happens to us when we die. All our energy just flies out of us.

(Spoon has become transfixed by the fire. Max, not sure how to participate in Spoon's reverie, walks to a window and looks out.)

MAX: Dark out there.

(Spoon says nothing. Max moves as if to go to the stairs, then tries the phone one more time. Obviously, nothing, he hangs up. Blackout.)

Scene 3

Morning. The living room fireplace is ablaze. Nicole is fussing around the kitchen, cleaning up nervously. Troy wanders up to her, reading from one of Max's books. Bread and coffee are laid out. The dirty dishes are there from the night before.

TROY: Did you know that Friedrich Nietzsche died of tertiary syphilis? Spent the last ten years of his life totally paralyzed and nuts. Just like Voltaire. Just like van Gogh. All the greats go mad.

NICOLE: Van Gogh. *(Pronounces it "van Gäk")*

TROY: What?

NICOLE: Van Gogh—the correct pronunciation is van Gogh. *(Again: "van Gäk")*

TROY *(Mimics her)*: Van Gäk! Got it, Nicole. We should do a book together. I need to get close to your editing prowess.

NICOLE: A book?

TROY: A novel. I just finished it. I'll give you across-the-board participation—movie rights, TV, whatever you want.

NICOLE *(Distracted)*: You wrote a novel?

TROY: I could have gone anywhere with it, but I wanted you to see it first. I have pages with me if you want to read them.

NICOLE: I don't think I can read anything right now.

TROY: Why not?

NICOLE: I have other things on my mind.

TROY: Like what?

NICOLE: Well, for one thing, this "power outage" was supposed to last two hours. It's been over ten. The cell phones won't lock on. All the food in the fridge is about to spoil. I dunno.

TROY: Put it out on the porch.

NICOLE: You cannot put caviar out on the porch.

TROY: Then I'll eat it now. For brunch.

(Troy picks up the caviar and eats it out of the tin. Nicole watches him with curious disgust.)

NICOLE: Doesn't this bother you?

TROY: Yes. It's an indecent violation of excellent caviar. But I have no choice. By the way, you're going to love my book. Why don't I read you the first chapter? I'll go grab the pages.

(Troy goes to his bedroom as Max enters the kitchen carrying a small sack of groceries. He throws car keys on the counter.)

MAX: Well, that didn't work out so great.

NICOLE: What happened?

MAX: I guess you need electricity to make the gas pumps work. *So* the gas station's closed. And there's no milk, no bread, no newspapers. No cash machine.

NICOLE: Did you talk to anyone?

(Troy enters with his pages. Seeing Max, he puts them down, continues eating caviar.)

MAX: The guy at the store—"Slim"—says it has nothing to do with a telephone pole. It's some kind of problem with "the grid." *(To Troy)* You two were up pretty late.

TROY: Oh, you heard us? We didn't flush.

MAX: Uh . . . no. I mean . . . never mind.

TROY: Oh, right. Sorry about that, she gets kind of loud, what can I say? At least she doesn't *bark*. I had a girlfriend once who sounded like a—

NICOLE: Wait a minute, *guys!* Max! "Grid"? What does . . . what does that mean? "Grid"?

MAX: I have no idea.

NICOLE: Well, why didn't you ask your buddy *Slim*?

MAX: Nicole, please take that tone out of your voice. I'm not one of your minions.

NICOLE: Maybe we should just pack up and go back to the city?

MAX: No way! We'll just take a ride down to that big grocery store, stock up. Then we'll be set.

NICOLE: Were you able to use the pay phone? Call Sara? Tell her what's happening? Or my mother? I should call my mother.

MAX: Pay phones are out, too. I tried to get some kind of news on the car radio, but all I got was static.

NICOLE: Static? . . .

MAX: There's only one station up here in the first place and they must need electricity, too.

TROY *(Twilight Zone theme)*: "Doo-doo-doo-doo, doo-doo-doo-doo."

MAX: Troy, *please!* *(Noticing)* What's that? The caviar?

TROY: Yes. It is. Want some? It's very good.

NICOLE: Max. What do you think?

MAX: I think we paid for the place. We're here now. Let's give it a chance.

NICOLE: But do you think it could be something like, you know, something someone *did*? On purpose?

(Troy pours himself a Stoli.)

TROY: Ever see that Henry Fonda movie *Fail-Safe*? He's talking on the phone to the prime minister of Russia and the atom bombs start dropping, and then there's this sound like: "BOOOOOOOOO." And someone says: "What's that sound?" And someone else says: "That's the sound of the phones melting in the fireball on the other end of the line."

MAX: Troy, that's not funny, OK? And it has nothing to do with what we're talking about.

TROY: Have a drink, Max. You're on vacation.

MAX: I don't drink in the morning. *(To Nicole)* Nicole, what are you saying?

NICOLE: Bet they have electricity in Saint Bart's.

MAX: That's not fair. You wanted to come up here as much as I did. In fact, it was *your* idea to go on this vacation.

NICOLE: There are a thousand places we could have gone.

MAX: And any one of them could have a blackout just like this. Jesus, Nicole!

(Spoon enters through the mudroom carrying a coal scuttle full of pinecones. She slips an arm around Troy and they kiss.)

SPOON: Good morning! *(Indicating the coal scuttle)* Check out what I've been collecting. They're all over the ground out there. *Millions*.

NICOLE: Those are called "pinecones." They fall off the pine trees.

SPOON: Uh, I *know* that. Duh.

MAX: I thought you were still in bed?

SPOON: On a day like this? I've been up since six. Look, they're so beautiful! Like little sculptures.

TROY: You hungry, baby? We have caviar.

SPOON: You guys have to get *outside*. The air is practically shimmering with sunshine. Everything is so alive! I saw a red fox and a bald eagle, I think it was a bald eagle, down by the pond. And the pond, it's like molten crystal. Everything is so still and perfect.

NICOLE: It's getting colder. We should stoke up the fireplace.

MAX: Got it.

(As Max moves toward the fireplace, Troy pulls out a joint from his pocket and lights it.)

TROY: Stoke up! Excellent idea.

MAX: Troy, it's eleven o'clock in the morning!

TROY: I know, it's getting late.

(Spoon takes the joint and toasts.)

SPOON: To nature, to serenity, to really getting away from it all. To pinecones. *(She tokes)*

MAX: I thought you didn't drink?

SPOON: Pot's herbal. Medicinal.

MAX *(Glum)*: True. I forgot about that part.

NICOLE: Max, the people at the store, did they look worried?

MAX: Well, they weren't very talkative, but no, they didn't look particularly concerned.

(The joint gets passed to Nicole, who takes it absentmindedly.)

NICOLE *(Toking)*: Yeah?

SPOON: Maybe there's a computer malfunction somewhere? All the electricity is routed by computer systems that regulate the flow of electricity through the grid.

MAX: The *grid*! You know what a grid is? *(Takes the joint from Nicole, tokes, passes it to Troy)*

SPOON: Everyone from California knows what a grid is. It's you know, where the electricity comes from.

NICOLE: OK, but Spoon, if this is because of some kind of problem with the "grid," then what does that have to do with the phones?

TROY: Phones need electricity don't they? Right? I mean, how *do* phones work, anyway? "Mr. Watson come here I need you." That's as far as I got.

SPOON *(Caressing Troy as she takes the joint from him)*: Phones are pretty simple. *(Takes a hit)* Sound waves cause the diaphragm to vibrate and the vibrations disturb a magnetic field which in turn induces an electrical current. *That's* transmitted to *another* phone causing the diaphragm in *it* to vibrate. *(Exhales a cloud of smoke)* Reproducing the original sound. See?

TROY: Isn't she great? *(They kiss)*

MAX *(Stoned)*: It *is* amazing when you think about it. Some unseen turbine hundreds of miles away fabricates all this energy, which courses over a vast, interlocking system of millions of fragile wires, continuously, silently, like an enormous river of electrons pulsing through a vast nerve network towards its destination, where it becomes power again, making the . . . the tiny blades of the coffee grinder spin.

TROY *(Mocking)*: Yeah, wow, man.

MAX: Shut up. I'm trying to be serious. Where does electricity come from anyway? Like where *is* the generator? I don't know. Do you? And what kind of generator is it? Nuclear? Coal? Do they use coal? Windmills? Maybe they just have this massive rubber band and they wind it up really, really tight . . .

SPOON: You know what it could be? *(Takes a huge hit)*

MAX: Tell us!

SPOON: A *storm*! Last year an enormous storm in the Midwest knocked out electricity, water and phones in four states.

MAX: But there's been no snow for weeks.

TROY: *Far away*, dude. Far, far away.

SPOON: Yeah, far, far, far away.

TROY: The old flapping-butterfly-wing-in-China routine.

MAX: The *what*?

TROY: You know, the butterfly wing flaps in China, makes a miniscule puff, which gets amplified until it's a flurry, then a breeze; one thing leads to the next, and by the time it gets here it's this enormo-destructo tornado.

(Beat.)

SPOON: It could be a million things. We live in a highly vulnerable social structure. One thing impacts on the next in a million ways. The currency exchange shifts, some country in Asia defaults on its loans, which affects a highly leveraged energy corporation like Enron—bing-bang, your lights go out.

MAX: How come when *I* smoke pot my IQ goes *down* and Spoon's goes *up*?

SPOON *(Getting into it)*: It could be something systemic affecting the population! Remember that movie with Dustin Hoffman and everyone had to wear space suits to prevent contamination from some insane virus?

TROY: *Outbreak.* Warner's. 1995. CAA package.

SPOON: Yeah. *Outbreak.* That was pretty crazy. That was sort of like this—small town, no one knows what's going on.

MAX: But that was totally fictional!

SPOON: Well what about anthrax? That's real. Terrorists are real. In 1984 the Soviet Union launched a smallpox outbreak that killed thousands of people in the middle of Siberia.

NICOLE *(Who has been following intently)*: That's right! There are scientists in Iran at this very moment, trying to create biowarfare cruise missiles. We did that book three years ago, the scariest thing I ever read. And what about Ebola, Max? That's the most contagious thing in the world. Zero survival rate.

MAX: Wait a minute, how do we get to bio-warfare from a power blackout?

TROY: Wouldn't that be a trip? The plague rampaging through the streets, causing havoc and chaos! Looting! Martial law!

MAX: This is absurd!

NICOLE: Wasn't it 1918 or 1919 when the flu killed all those people? Like twenty million, was it twenty million? *(Stoned)* Twenty million?

TROY: Twenty million, that sounds about right.

NICOLE: Or was it thirty?

SPOON: It *was* thirty. Definitely thirty. *(Beat)* Wow. That would so screw things up.

(Beat.)

NICOLE: It's so quiet all of a sudden.

(Overwhelming silence.)

I want to call my mother.

MAX: Nicole . . .

(Nicole stands, panicky.)

NICOLE: Shit. I can't tell whether I'm stoned or if I'm having an anxiety attack.

TROY: I have Prozac if you want it.

MAX: You're on Prozac?

TROY: No, I just have it. You know, in case I want to see things from a different perspective.

SPOON: I saw this movie where this terrorist brought a small nuclear device into the city in a *rowboat*. That could happen *so* easily. Probably just a matter of time.

NICOLE: Stop for a sec, Spoon, please?

MAX: Nicole, you OK?

NICOLE: I just need some fresh air.

(Nicole moves to go out but doesn't leave.)

NAT *(Off)*: Hello!

MAX: Oh, jeez, it's Nat. Troy, throw the joint in the fireplace.

NICOLE: Oh, I can't deal with this guy right now!

(Nat enters carrying jugs of water.)

NAT: How we all doin'? We hanging in there?

MAX: Oh, hey, Nat, hey, come on in.

TROY *(Jovial)*: Hey, Nat! How's the sheep farm?

NAT: Sheep?! No sheep around this way. You guys getting by without the cable TV?

MAX: Pretty well. You?

NAT: Oh, I dunno. We lose the juice up here so often, it doesn't really affect us. *(Beat)* I brought you some water and candles. Should hold you a couple of days.

NICOLE: Couple of days?!

NAT: From what I've heard, there's been a big storm about two hundred miles north of here . . .

TROY: Flap, flap.

MAX *(Ignoring Troy)*: Yeah?

NAT: And a big transformer or something blew out. That's what the state troopers are telling everybody. Probably take a couple of days to fix.

MAX: A storm. Really? *(To Nat)* A transformer? Hmmm.

NAT: That's what they say. Why, you hear something different?

NICOLE: We thought it could be, you know, something serious.

NAT: Like what?

TROY: The end of the world, something along those lines.

NAT: Nope. Sorry. I didn't hear anything like that.

MAX: How many towns are affected?

NAT: Pretty much all the towns.

NICOLE: What's "all the towns"?

NAT: All the towns in the county. Next county, too, so they say.

NICOLE: So what's going to happen? I mean what are people doing about it?

NAT: Ah, people lived up here for hundreds of years without electricity. We can get by for a few days. You got food and somebody to keep you warm, what else do you need? What *is* that smell?

TROY: Weed. You want some?

NAT: Weed? *(Beat)* Sure, why not?

(Troy resuscitates the joint, lights it. They pass the joint around.)

TROY: Check this shit out. This is the shit Kevin Spacey smoked in *American Beauty*.

NICOLE: A few days. That's not so good. Max?

MAX: You hear anything on the radio, Nat?

NAT: Radio? Radio's out, no electricity.

NICOLE: "Radio's out." Great.

TROY: So, Nat, what do you do up here for fun? You hunt?

NAT: Not really, no time. In fact, I gotta get up some fencing before the first snow, or the deer'll eat all the shrubs right down. They love those rhodie buds, munch on 'em like candy.

TROY: Yeah. They do. *(Pause)* What's a "rhodie bud"?

NAT: You know, flowers. Have to do the gutters, too. I'll wait till you guys leave.

MAX: Gutters?

NAT: Well, this time of year, the roof gutters get all filled up with pine needles, then snow piles up on 'em. Next thing you know, you got the ice creepin' up under your shingles and a leaky roof. Every year I get the calls: "Nat, help! I got a leaky roof." And I wanna say: "Why don't you cut down that friggin' pine tree you got hanging over your gutters!" You know? Pardon my French. *(Laughs)* People don't think. They plant the trees right up next to the house, roots clog the plumbing, squirrels get in the attic. If I had my way, I'd get out the chain saw, cut 'em all down. Toss 'em in the chipper. *(Taking a hit)* This stuff's almost as good as Zeke's.

(Nat gets more animated and relaxed. The group is transfixed.)

MAX: "Zeke"?

NAT: Has about an acre of pot behind his chicken sheds. Chicken poop is one hell of a fertilizer.

TROY: Yup. I've always found that to be true.

SPOON: Don't the police do anything?

NAT: Only police around here are staties, and they stick to the thruway.

NICOLE: Oh.

NAT: It's pretty much live and let live up here. Lots of people who like their privacy: hippies, hillbillies.

NICOLE: Hillbillies?

NAT: Oh, yeah, you know, with the overalls and the long beards? Make pies out of woodchucks. You mind if I . . . ? *(Indicates fruit bowl)*

NICOLE *(Laughs a crazy laugh)*: No, no. Go ahead. These hillbillies, how close are they?

(Nat takes an apple and kicks back.)

NAT: Five miles? Two miles? Couldn't say, they're up there in the woods. They're like the bikers; they keep to themselves.

TROY: Bikers?

NAT *(Laughing)*: Oh sure. They're a riot. There's this one big dude, Mal? Has a swastika tattooed right in the middle of his forehead.

MAX: This is a buddy of yours?

NAT: Hell *no!* In fact, two years ago he was beating on his girl-friend at the volunteer firemen's Fourth of July barbecue and I grabbed him, right? He took a bite right out of my side.

SPOON: He bit you? With his teeth? That must have hurt.

NAT: It's OK, I just chucked his head right into the cinder block wall, knocked him out cold. *(Smiling)* We all ended up going to the hospital together.

(Nicole, who has grown very quiet, retreats to a corner.)

SPOON: Wow.

TROY: Nothing like a firemen's barbecue for a good time.

NAT: That's true. *(Noticing Nicole)* Are you OK?

NICOLE: Me? Oh, I'm fine . . .

MAX: Thanks for the water, Nat.

NAT: Sure. Sure. *(Beat)* Well, I better get going. Mom's waiting lunch for me. *(Gets up. As he passes Nicole)* Bye.

NICOLE: Bye. And thanks, Nat.

NAT: No problem.

(Nat's gone.)

MAX: Nicole? You all right?

(Nicole finds a Yellow Pages. She starts flipping through it.)

SPOON: See, it's no biggie. So why don't we all get some fresh air and chill?

TROY: Yeah, let's go see that molten crystal pond. Max?

(Troy and Spoon move to the door. Nicole finds what she needs, picks up the phone.)

NICOLE: *Yes!* Dial tone. See? Positive thinking. *(Dials, listens)*

MAX: Phone's working?

NICOLE: "All circuits are busy." Fuck! *(Pushes more buttons)* Maybe it's only long distance that's screwed up.

MAX: Who could you possibly be calling?

NICOLE: Yeah, hi, could I? OK. *(To Max)* Now I'm on hold.

MAX: Who are you calling, Nicole?

NICOLE *(Into phone)*: Is this the Marriott? Yeah, hi, I want to make a reservation for . . . *(Listening)* I know, I know, we're about twenty miles from you, we have the same problem that's why . . . Uh, OK. *(To Max)* I'm not just going to sit here, Max.

MAX: Nicole.

SPOON: I hate those big hotel chains.

TROY: Sweetness, there are no Four Seasons this far from civilization. *(To Nicole)* Make sure they have goose-down pillows.

NICOLE: I'm holding. Yes, I understand but . . . excuse me, may I finish? I am a platinum card holder and I . . . I know that, I understand that, you have no rooms for tonight, but what I'm saying is, yes . . . My company spends a lot of money on lodging and I'm just saying, I need a *room* tonight, two rooms actually and I would appreciate . . . Yes, I'll hold.

MAX: Nicole, we don't need a room. And besides she's not going to help you out.

NICOLE *(To Max)*: YES SHE *IS*!!! If she doesn't have a room, she has to tell me where I can find one. That's part of the "platinum executive program." *(To phone)* . . . Hello? Hello? Yes? I know that, I understand that, that has been explained to me *twice now.* But . . .

MAX: We have a perfectly good place right here.

NICOLE *(Gritted teeth; to Max)*: Max! *(To phone)* What? No, I wasn't speaking to you. But *no*, don't put me on hold. Well, you *asked* me and I'm saying don't. *(Listens; then suddenly subdued)* What? But, how can you . . . ? Oh, then . . . thank you.

(Nicole gently hangs the phone up. Max picks it up and listens.)

MAX: Line's dead. No dial tone at all now.

(In a funk, Nicole walks over and slumps onto the couch.)

NICOLE: We can't get a room because they're going to close the hotel tomorrow.

MAX: Close the hotel? How can they do that?

NICOLE: The whole region is without electricity. Some vacation.

TROY: I've got the munchies and I'm making lunch, who's hungry?

NICOLE: Those dishes aren't clean.

TROY: Clean enough. How about crabmeat salad everyone? Use up the mayo. In another six hours it won't be mayo anymore, it will be deadly poison. *(No response)* I take that as a yes.

SPOON: C'mon, it's really beautiful outside, let's go for that walk, then have lunch?

(No one responds. Troy continues to bustle about.)

TROY *(Singing)*: ". . . The end of the world as we know it."
NICOLE: Troy, please wash those dishes before using them.
SPOON: It's so nice out!

(Nicole crowds Troy, who is now opening the cans of crabmeat with a can opener.)

NICOLE: Are you washing those or just rinsing?
TROY: Nicole, relax.
NICOLE: I'm just saying that if you're cleaning, it's usually a wise idea to use some kind of dishwashing detergent.
TROY: Oh, is it? I didn't know that. Any particular brand?
NICOLE: Just, just . . . you know what? Just leave all that and I'll do it later.
TROY: No, really I'm curious. Why is this so important to you?
NICOLE: To kill the germs!
TROY: What germs?
SPOON *(Trying not to be amused)*: Troy, stop it!
MAX: Nicole, let's all go for a walk?
TROY: What germs? Where?
NICOLE: Germs. Germs! *Germs*, you know? Louis Pasteur? Modern science? Sanitation?
TROY: This is very bourgeois of you, Nicole.

(Nicole jumps up, pushes Troy away from the sink.)

Well, excuse me!

(Nicole takes the dishes Troy just "washed" and puts them back in the sink. She begins frenetically cleaning.)

MAX: Lemme help with that.

NICOLE: No! I'm fine. Really.

> *(Nicole grabs the crabmeat can, misjudges the distance, and cuts her hand on the lid. Blood drips onto the counter.)*

NICOLE: Ow!!! SHIT!

TROY: Did you cut yourself?

NICOLE: Yes, you asshole!

TROY: Oh, is that blood?

NICOLE: Get away from me!

> *(Nicole whirls away from Troy, now spilling the crabmeat salad all over the floor.)*

Shit!

TROY: My salad!

> *(Nicole wraps her hand, there's blood staining the white towel.)*

MAX: Nicole, that doesn't look so good.

> *(Max runs upstairs to the bathroom.)*

SPOON: Nicole, let me see it.

NICOLE *(Maddened)***:** NO!!! Everyone go away!

TROY: That's a lot of blood.

> *(Max flies back down the stairs.)*

MAX: All they've got are these Band-Aids and Neosporin. Let me see it, Nicole.

TROY: Do you want me to finish doing the dishes?

MAX: TROY, WILL YOU SHUT THE FUCK UP!

> *(Nicole curls over, weeping softly.)*

Honey, it'll be all right. Come on, there must be a hospital
around here somewhere. We'll have a doctor look at it.

NICOLE: What hospital? Where?

MAX: I don't know, we'll ask them at Slim's.

SPOON: Maybe we should call Nat.

MAX: Right.

(Max picks up the house phone. Listens.)

Still nothing.

(Max picks up Troy's cell phone, punches numbers, listens.)

Damn it!

(Max throws the phone, shattering it.)

TROY: That thing was state-of-the-art.

MAX: That's not what's important at the moment, is it, Troy?

TROY: Well, uh, yeah, it is. What do we do without a phone?

MAX: Nicole's cell.

NICOLE: My battery's dead.

SPOON: Mine, too.

MAX: LOOK, I DON'T KNOW! Let's deal with one thing at a time.
Come on Nicole, let's just go.

NICOLE: What if we run out of gas? You said there's no gas stations.

MAX: We have enough gas to find a hospital.

NICOLE: What if we get lost? Or get a flat tire? Or they can't see me
right away and we get stuck driving back in the dark and a
bunch of bikers find us? Or hillbillies?

MAX: That's not going to happen.

NICOLE: I think it's stopped bleeding.

MAX: Are you sure?

NICOLE: I don't want to go driving around right now, OK?

SPOON: I don't know about you, but I'm still a little high. I don't
really want to go where there are, you know, people.

MAX: Should we wait for a while?

SPOON: Wait, see how it's feeling.

MAX: Yeah. That's a plan. If it starts to feel worse.

TROY: Remember that movie *Deliverance*? *(Mimics banjo picking)*

SPOON: Troy, come outside with me.

TROY: What?

(Troy and Spoon leave as Max stands over Nicole, protective.)

MAX: OK.

NICOLE: OK. *(Long beat)* Max, I want to go.

MAX: To the hospital?

NICOLE: No. I want to go home. I want to leave.

MAX: That doesn't really make sense, Nicole. I mean: (A) I'm not
sure we can find gas; (B) Do you really want to drive for
hours and maybe run the risk of getting stuck somewhere?
Hotels are closing. There's no electricity for miles around.
I mean, we're here. What's the big deal?

NICOLE: Two days?

MAX: What if I told you that you only had to endure this for
another twelve hours? Would you do it?

NICOLE: Max, that's not the point.

MAX: Twenty-four hours? Thirty-six hours? I mean, we've gone
on camping trips that were much more difficult than this.
Everyone's just getting very wound-up.

NICOLE: Don't tell me I'm wound-up.

MAX: Look, this isn't pleasant. But it's not the end of the world.

NICOLE: How do you know?

MAX: Nicole. You heard Nat, it's a broken transformer.

NICOLE: That's what someone said.

MAX: Tomorrow, maybe the day after, we'll know more. And when
we do, we can decide then. Right now, our best bet is to throw
some logs on the fire and kick back. Right? It'll be good to
live without a phone for a couple of days. We've never done

this. Really spent time together like this. It's not a big deal. They'll fix it.

NICOLE: Yeah.

MAX: Remember, the things you worry about the most never happen.

NICOLE: I wasn't worrying about this.

(Nicole looks at her hand, stands, then goes upstairs to the bathroom. Max, unsure of what to do next, goes down and checks the fireplace. They are out of firewood. He walks up to the mudroom. He finds an ax there and takes it outside. We hear the sound of wood splitting as the lights go down.)

ACT TWO

Scene 1

One week later. Daylight. The sound of an ax splitting wood mingled with dogs barking. Stacks of empty egg cartons and plastic water jugs. Guttered candles have dripped wax over every surface. The face of the fireplace is stained with soot. Pinecones and pine boughs decorate every edge and surface of the room.

Spoon sits at the table wearing a fuzzy overcoat, drinking glasses of something she pours from an unlabeled plastic jug. The sound of chopping stops. Max, wearing an old parka and sporting a week's worth of beard stubble, enters hauling an armload of wood. He throws it by the fireplace.

MAX: Fucking dogs out there. Hanging around.

SPOON: I think they're abandoned. I gave them some eggs to eat.

MAX: Great. Tomorrow there'll be twice as many.

SPOON: Have some of Nat's cider. It's good. He calls it "applejack."

(Max rummages for food in the kitchen.)

MAX: Where's the homemade peanut butter?
SPOON: Troy finished it two days ago.

(Nicole comes out of the bedroom and groggily heads for the bathroom. Her hand is bandaged.)

MAX: Fuck! I can't eat another egg. *(To Nicole)* It's one o'clock in the afternoon, Nicole.

(Nicole doesn't reply, she slams the door.)

(To Spoon) She stays up all night and sleeps all day.
SPOON: You know, it's funny, I *like* eggs. I think we're lucky to have 'em, you know? And the stove works, so that's a good thing. I mean, this isn't that bad. Is it? The weather's nice and clear and crispy. We're surrounded by nature and woods and all that stuff. And there's no phones. No agents or publicists calling up all day long. Can't go shopping. Can't do anything but just, you know, be calm. I like this. I like this a lot. I don't think I've felt this clear in a long long time. You know? I get up early. I do my yoga. I go for walks. I breathe fresh air all day. I watch the clouds in the sky. I can think. And when it gets dark I go to bed. It's like a dream come true. Back in L.A., all I do is get stuck in traffic and talk on my cell phone and use my credit card and worry about my career. I needed this. I really, really needed this.

(Nicole emerges from the bathroom. Comes down to the kitchen, gets a kettle, fills it from a jug of water, puts it on the stove. She favors her good hand. Max watches her, she ignores him.)

MAX: I could use some help you know.
NICOLE: Max, please don't start. I just woke up.

SPOON: Good morning, Nicole. I mean, good afternoon.

MAX: If you went to bed on time . . .

NICOLE: How am I supposed to help you when I have this? *(Holds up her hand)*

MAX: We should have had those stitches out two days ago.

NICOLE: I'm not going back there, Max. Can you imagine what that place is like now? Like something you see on the evening news! All those pathetic people lined up. Babies crying. And what do you think that hospital smells like now, a week later? I don't want some local yokel country doctor who's had two hours of sleep screwing around with my hand. I need my hand, it's useful. OK? I'll deal with the stitches when we get home.

MAX: Does it still hurt?

NICOLE: *I don't want to talk about it right now.* OK? Can I have five minutes to myself before you start nagging me?

MAX *(Resigned)***:** I'm not nagging you.

NICOLE: Go do your frontiersman bit and chop your wood. Go swing your big ax.

(Spoon snickers. Max gives her a hateful look. Troy rushes in, carrying bags of groceries, throws them down.)

TROY: I just got stopped at a *checkpoint*.

MAX: "Checkpoint"? What do you mean "checkpoint"?

TROY: So I stop. And this one redneck comes over and says: "Sir, please step out of your vehicle and stand to one side."

SPOON: He was a cop?

TROY: I don't know. They had *guns*, Spoon! What was I going to do? Run over them? Give 'em an excuse to fine-tune the crosshairs on their rifle scopes?

MAX: That's nuts.

TROY: So I get out of the car while this jerk checks my license and registration. Then another one with a crew cut and an army jacket, you know, Special Forces wannabe, sidles up and wants to know what I'm *doing* around here. How come I'm so far from California? I tell him I'm on vacation. That gets him even more wound up. Wants to know how much I'm renting the place for, who else is up here with me? I told him it was none of his fucking business.

MAX: Oh, jeez! **NICOLE:** Troy!

TROY: Oh yeah. Guy gives me this long look like he's going to *do* something. What's he going to *do*? Arrest me? Beat me up?

MAX: You shouldn't push it, Troy.

TROY: Ah, fuck him. Fuck all of 'em. Did your buddy Nat stop by today?

MAX: He's not my buddy.

TROY: Sure he is. Mister Authenticity. Laughing at us behind our backs.

MAX: The guy has been very helpful.

TROY: The guy is having the time of his life.

(Troy starts unpacking all kinds of groceries from the bags.)

I can see him hanging out with all his pals. Laughing about the fools from the city stuck up at the Murphy place, freezing their nuts off, chewing on pinecones.

MAX: That's the way you see it. That's just your prejudice against him.

TROY: Yeah? Before I got stopped? There was this bonfire down by a little league field. So I figure I'll go down and see if anyone had any news. And by the fire all these local guys are hunched over this, I don't know what it was, maybe a cow carcass, maybe a moose, I don't know, sawing at it with knives. Chopping off the legs, the neck. Not talking, just kind of hacking and grunting. Blood smeared all over their pants, their jackets. I could smell the steaming guts spilled all over the dirt. One of 'em was working on the throat, totally focused, the sweat dripping off his nose, a

cigarette hanging from his lips. His hands covered in gore.
I must have been staring at him. He looked up at me, and
I realized, this guy hates me. He doesn't know me, but he
hates me, because he knows I don't belong here. I left.
Just got in the car and left.

MAX: This is you, Troy. This is you projecting all of this on these
people. On Nat. Nat hasn't done a thing to you.

TROY: Yet.

NICOLE (*Focused on Troy's unpacking*): What's all this?

TROY: Hey, I don't know about you, but I need my coffee in the
morning. So I went and got some. Plus I found frozen steaks.
Chocolate-covered potato chips. You'd be amazed what's
out there.

MAX: "Found"?

TROY: There are empty summer homes all over the place up here.
Those people don't need this stuff. *We* do.

(*Troy focuses on Spoon for the first time.*)

Whatcha drinking there, Spoon?

SPOON: This is cider.

TROY: *Hard* cider, my dear. As in "alcoholic beverage."

SPOON: Don't patronize me, Troy. OK?

TROY: I never patronize you, Spoon.

SPOON: Leave me alone. If I want to drink hard cider, I'll drink it.
I really resent you mocking me in front of everybody.
Treating me like some kind of bimbo.

TROY: Stop acting like a bimbo and I'll stop treating you like one.

SPOON: How do I act like a bimbo? Tell me! *How?*

TROY: The whole sunny, positive bit. Always smiling like you don't
have a thought in your head. It's getting old. It's getting
really, really boring.

SPOON: At least I don't bitch and moan all day like you. *That's*
what's boring. *You're* the one who's boring. Is it my fault
that I'm not suffering like you are?

TROY: Yes. It is. Because you're too dim-witted to notice how fucked-up this all is. And that's depressing.

MAX: Troy, take a Prozac.

TROY: I don't need a Prozac. *(Continuing his rant)* Sitting on your ass, meditating, doing yoga. I'm out there finding food. Finding gas. What are you doing? Nothing. You think this is fun! This is your idea of a good time. Fresh air! Pine-cones! Baby rabbits! I hate this. I HATE IT!

SPOON: Troy, don't yell at me.

TROY: I'm not yelling at you.

SPOON: My father used to yell at me. I will not be yelled at.

TROY: Please don't start sharing about your traumatic childhood.

(Spoon is on the verge of tears.)

And don't start crying, it's repulsive.

SPOON: No one's crying! *You're* the one who wanted to come on this, this whatever it is, "vacation." This was *your* agenda! And you didn't get what you wanted, so now you've turned into a total asshole.

MAX: Let's all calm down.

TROY: Spoon, just shut up and drink your cider.

SPOON: Hey, Max, you know why your best friend came on this vacation? To hang with his homies? He wants to sell his new novel to Nicole.

TROY: You're right, Spoon. You shouldn't drink, you become delusional.

SPOON: Did you tell Max about your novel?

MAX: You have a novel, Troy? *(To Nicole)* Did Troy tell you about a novel?

TROY: I just wanted Nicole to give me some input. I wasn't ready to . . . uh . . .

MAX: Oh. Well, I'll read it. Whenever. *(Beat)* I was wondering why you came. I thought, I have so few real friends in the world.

I can depend on Troy. He seems like a jerk, but he's real.
He's my "best friend."

TROY: I *am* your friend. To the degree that anyone is a friend to anyone.

MAX: We need more wood.

(Max heads for the door.)

TROY: You may be smarter than me, Max, but I'm the one who gets it done. I get it done, Max, because I'm not afraid to make a move.

(Max goes out. We hear him chopping. Nicole picks up her tea and goes back up to the bedroom. Troy yells up to her.)

Nicole, I only wanted you to see it first!

(Nicole closes the door. Beat.)

Thanks, Spoon.

SPOON: I'm sorry.

(Troy unplugs the TV and carries it to the kitchen. Then he starts to pack odds and ends into a box.)

(Watching him) What are you doing?

TROY: We should have left a week ago.

SPOON: Where are you taking the TV?

TROY: It's called barter.

SPOON: But there's no gas.

TROY: There's gas.

SPOON: One gallon at a time. Where are we going to go on one gallon?

TROY: To the next gas station.

SPOON: Troy, you don't even know if there *is* another gas station.

TROY: Of course there's another gas station! Do you think it's like this a hundred miles from here? This is just some fucked-up place.

SPOON *(Puts her face in her hands)*: But we don't . . . you don't even know if the roads are open.

(Troy relents, touches her shoulder.)

TROY: Hey . . . *(To himself)* What am I doing here? My hands are covered with blisters from chopping. My shoes, my beautiful shoes, are encrusted with mud and deer shit. These shoes cost three hundred and fifty dollars, look at them.

SPOON: They're just shoes.

TROY: No. They're *me*. I'm letting myself go. I stink. I'm hungry and tired all the time. So cold I can't think straight. I have to get out of here.

SPOON: In a few days . . .

TROY: No. Not in a few days. Right now. I'm leaving.

SPOON: Troy. Whatever this is, we can get through it together.

TROY: No. *You* get through it. I shouldn't even be here. I should be in L.A. Right now. Right this minute, I should be sitting in a warm, spotless restaurant. Scrubbed floor, clean hands, sipping bottled water, perusing a menu, a waiter at my side, eagerly awaiting my decision. *(Addressing an invisible waiter)* Yes, I'd like to start with the tapenade, and follow that with the mesclun salad lightly sprinkled with a dressing of grapeseed oil and rare balsamic vinegar. Oh, warm sourdough breadsticks! Awesome. And yes, I'll have the grilled Chilean sea bass on the bed of marinated artichokes and roasted portobello mushrooms. What's that? I think you're right, Rothschild '87. Excellent choice.

(Spoon embraces Troy from behind.)

SPOON: Baby, let's go to bed. You'll feel better.

TROY: No I won't.

SPOON: You will.

TROY: I don't want to.

SPOON: Because you think I'm repulsive?

(Troy breaks away and continues packing up the things he's taking.)

TROY: People get what they deserve. I'm not waiting around for the other shoe to drop.

(Troy moves to the door with the boxes.)

SPOON: I want to come with you.

TROY: I'll be back after I gas up.

SPOON: Promise?

TROY: Hey . . .

(Troy kisses her quickly, then leaves.

Spoon pours herself a large glass of cider, finds a forgotten bottle of vodka, pours a shot into the glass, and knocks it back. She lights a cigarette. Then she gets up and walks to the windows. She watches Max chop. She returns to the table just as he enters with the wood.

Max goes to the fire and stokes it up. Spoon walks over to him.)

SPOON: You make such a pretty fire, Max.

MAX: Thanks.

(Spoon touches Max's shoulder.)

SPOON: You want a drink?

MAX: Not right now.

SPOON: It'll make you feel better.

MAX: What's the saying: "This too shall pass"?

SPOON: I love that saying.

MAX *(Beat):* Yeah. Well, this'll be over soon. *(Looking)* Where's the TV?

SPOON: Max. Could you do me a favor?

MAX: Sure.

SPOON: Could you give me a hug?

MAX: A hug?

SPOON: Just hold me. For a sec. Please?

MAX: Sure.

(Max stands and faces Spoon. He hugs her. The hug lasts a little too long.)

SPOON: You're such a sweet guy, Max. You know that? I like you. I like you a lot.

MAX: I like you, too.

(Max pulls himself from Spoon's embrace.)

Watch out, I might think you're trying to seduce me.

(Spoon says nothing—that is what she's doing. Uncomfortable pause as they both realize that.

Nicole emerges from the bedroom, walks down to the kitchen, pours some hot water from the kettle into her cup, and returns to her room.)

Troy wrote a book?

SPOON: Uh-huh.

MAX: What's it about?

SPOON: It's autobiographical. All about his crazy family and his crazy childhood.

MAX: I didn't know Troy had a crazy childhood.

SPOON: He was very poor. Brought up in foster homes.

MAX: No way! I went to college with the guy, believe me, I know.
SPOON: Maybe he just never told you.

(Spoon finds her jacket and slips it on. She heads for the door.)

MAX: Yeah. Maybe he didn't. Where are you going?
SPOON: Nowhere. Just for a walk.
MAX: Well, don't go too far. It's getting late.

(Spoon is almost out the door.)

Where is Troy anyway?
SPOON: Out driving, I guess.
MAX: Do you know when he's coming back?
SPOON: No. —Hey, it's starting to snow. That's cool. I love snow.

(Spoon goes out. Long beat. Max goes to the door.)

MAX: Spoon? Spoon? Wait a second.

*(Max grabs his coat and leaves.
Lights fade.)*

Scene 2

It's dark now. Candles and the fireplace illuminate the space. Nicole sits at the large oak table. Before her is an egg, which she spins with her good hand. She's drinking the hard cider. Max enters the kitchen, tosses his car keys on the counter.

MAX: Can't find her. Looked everywhere. Did Troy come back?
NICOLE: Troy's not coming back, Max. Isn't that obvious?
MAX: No. Nothing's obvious.

NICOLE *(Flat)*: When I get home, I'm taking a long, hot bath. In fact I don't think I'll ever get out. *(Beat)* I wonder if Billy made the deadline?

(Beat. Sound of a gun being fired off.)

MAX: What's that?

NICOLE *(Flat)*: Hunters I guess. Getting closer.

(Another gunshot.
Max goes to the living room and plays with the fire. He throws in a log. Nicole stands. She's unsteady on her feet. She picks up her egg and wanders over to Max.)

I love eggs. I wish we had *more* eggs.

MAX *(Offhand)*: I don't.

(Nicole holds her egg up for inspection.)

NICOLE: You know what I love about eggs?

MAX: What?

(Nicole tosses the egg in the air, catches it, tosses it, catches it.)

NICOLE: They're so perfect. Perfect . . . but . . .

(Nicole lets the egg drop onto the floor. It breaks.)

MAX: Oh, shit.

(Nicole takes another egg from the carton, tosses it up and down.)

NICOLE: Did you know, you can put a hundred pounds of pressure on an egg like this . . . *(She pinches the egg from top and bottom)* . . . and it won't break? Won't. Very strong. A marvel of physics and construction.

MAX: Nicole.

NICOLE: An egg can take a huge, an incredible amount of pressure. I think I heard somewhere that if you place an egg the right way, you can run over it with a steamroller and it won't break. Or was it hit it with a sledgehammer? No that can't be it.

MAX: I never heard that. Have you been drinking?

NICOLE: No, I haven't been drinking! Wait, I got it wrong. An *elephant*, something with an elephant. An elephant can step on an egg and it won't crack. Isn't that amazing? That an egg could withstand that kind of pressure?

MAX: Nicole.

NICOLE: It is amazing. *But*, if you drop it— *(Lets go of the egg)* The egg gets all fucked-up.

(Max grabs some paper towels and cleans up the mess.)

MAX: Please.

(Nicole drops another egg next to Max.)

NICOLE: So fragile.

(Nicole drops another egg. Max grabs her wrists.)

MAX: Nicole. Nicole. Stop!

(Nicole won't meet his eyes.)

NICOLE: "Humpty Dumpty sat on a wall . . ."

(Max holds onto her wrists.)

MAX: Nicole!
NICOLE: Let go!

MAX: Stop it. You're scaring me!

(Nicole tears her wrists from Max and walks away.)

NICOLE: Scaring *you*? You're out there somewhere, who knows if you're ever coming back or what! I'm here all alone. Someone's out there with a shotgun. And my HAND HURTS, Max!!!

MAX: OK, OK. Calm down!

NICOLE: Let's go *now*!

MAX: We can't go home now. We need gas.

NICOLE: Just pay whatever we have to pay. Sell whatever we have to sell.

MAX: But we don't know what's going on back home. Maybe they're in a blackout, too? We haven't seen a newspaper, heard a radio, nothing for six days. We can't just go back. Not yet.

NICOLE: So we just stay here for what? Another week? A month? Two months? A year?

MAX: Don't be ridiculous. This isn't going to last a month!

(The sound of barking dogs.)

NICOLE: Why aren't the phones working, Max? Why isn't there any news?

MAX: Someone said they saw some National Guardsmen. So they'll tell us what to do.

NICOLE: Will they? Max, maybe they've been lying all along because they don't want people to panic, to make trouble. They're trying to control this situation. Maybe that's why the soldiers are here.

MAX: Who's "they"?

NICOLE: The people in charge. The government. "Homeland Security"! Do you think for a second, if something really bad happened, that they would want us to know about it? You think if there was some kind of massive terrorist attack

they would let us in on it? THEY DON'T WANT US TO
KNOW!

MAX: Nicole! Nicole! You're being paranoid. You have to get a
grip on yourself.

NICOLE: But Max, admit it's a possibility!

MAX: OK, look, if by some wild stretch of the imagination something *has* happened out there, it's the last place on earth
I want to be. And . . . and . . . We *don't* know. No one
knows. Do you? I mean . . . look, we get out on the road
and there's no telling what we'll run into. It's all strangers
out there.

NICOLE: It's all strangers *here*, Max. We don't know anybody *here*.
We're totally cut off. No phones. No one's taking credit
cards. And what happens when we run out of cash? When
we run out of food?

MAX: We'll cross that bridge when we get to it.

NICOLE: We're crossing the bridge now! Right now! We are on the
bridge and the bridge is very rickety and scary. Don't you
see that?

MAX: No! Don't be so dramatic. I'm just trying to figure out the
best way—

NICOLE: *Fuck* the best way. This isn't something you take a poll
on! You have to be decisive. Because I'll tell you something, in case you don't know . . . This "situation" is not a
stable situation. There are men at checkpoints. *Men.* With
guns. And when men get together, shitty things happen.

MAX: Give it two more days.

NICOLE: Don't you care what happens to us? Or could happen to
me? Aren't you afraid?

MAX: No, because I refuse to panic.

NICOLE: Max, being smart doesn't count around here. Whether
you like it or not. This isn't Scrabble. This is a whole different rule book. *(Beat)* Two more days, two more weeks.
It's only going to get worse.

MAX: No. You're wrong. I know you're wrong.

(Nat appears in the mudroom carrying a carton and a shotgun. He tries the door and finds it locked. He taps lightly. Max opens the door for him.)

NAT: Good idea locking the door.

MAX: You been hunting, Nat? We heard a gun.

NAT: Not me.

MAX: But . . . *(Indicating shotgun)*

NAT: Oh, uh, no, this is my dad's. I don't know, seems to make sense to carry it. I can leave it in the truck if it bothers you.

MAX: No. It's fine.

(Nat props the shotgun up against the wall. Nicole goes to the table and sits. Nat puts the carton he's carrying on the table, then pours himself a glass of cider.)

NAT: So . . . How we all doin'? Hanging in there?

MAX: I could use a hot shower, but we seem to be OK.

(Nicole laughs sarcastically, as in: "Speak for yourself.")

NAT: Zeke sent over some more eggs. And my mom threw in some of her canned beets. A loaf of bread. Candles. And clean water. I don't know how much of that pond water you should be drinking.

MAX: We boil it.

NAT: Guy in a truck was giving out all these unlabeled tins. Got to be something good in there. But if it smells like tuna it's probably cat food.

NICOLE: You want to sit down, Nat?

NAT: No. Thanks. I'll just unpack this stuff. There's a meeting down by the firehouse. Folks from around here trying to figure out what we're going to do.

NICOLE: What are people saying?

NAT: Well, I met a guy yesterday who said he saw some National Guardsmen going by in trucks.

MAX: Yeah. We heard something about that. I guess that's a good thing, right?

NAT: You know what they say: "This too shall pass."

NICOLE: Is that what they say?

MAX: We need wood.

(Max takes a hurricane lantern and exits. Nat picks up the jug of hard cider.)

NAT: My great-grandma's recipe.

NICOLE: Yes. Delicious. *(Beat)* Must have been wonderful growing up here.

NAT: Kind of boring, actually. A lot of hard work for a kid. Up before school, milking. Shoveling cow shit. Sterilizing milk cans. Checking the feed. Shoveling more shit. I hated shoveling shit.

NICOLE: But it must have been kind of peaceful.

NAT: You ever try to shove a cow through a lye bath? Nothing peaceful about a half ton of meat trying to kick your skull in.

NICOLE: Your family had a farm?

NAT: Used to. Belonged to my great-grandpa. Had twelve kids, but a bunch of 'em got the flu after World War I and died. They're all buried over in Waterville. One of the gravestones just says "baby." Never even had a name.

NICOLE: "Baby"?

NAT: Yup. She would have been my mom's auntie I guess, if she had lived. But she didn't.

NICOLE: A baby with no name. That is so sad.

NAT: This is gonna sound silly, but every once in a while, I put flowers on the grave.

NICOLE: Do you have a girlfriend, Nat?

NAT: No. Not really.

NICOLE: You should. You're a nice man.

NAT *(Smiling)*: You think so?

(Nicole pours herself more cider and sips it.)

NICOLE: You must think we're a bunch of assholes.

NAT: No, of course not.

NICOLE: You do.

(Nicole starts to cry. At first Nat isn't sure what she's doing, then when he figures it out, he's not sure how to react.)

NAT: Uh . . .

(Nat approaches Nicole, wanting to console her. Finally he pats her shoulder. She touches his hand. A long moment. Finally, Nicole pulls away and wipes her nose. She stands and gathers herself.)

NICOLE: I'm sorry. *(Blowing her nose, etc.)* Look at me. In the city they call me the Dragon Lady.

(Nat notices her awkward use of her hand.)

NAT: How's your hand?

NICOLE: It hurts. They told me I had to go back to the hospital, but I'm afraid they're going to tell me that it's infected. It hurts . . . a lot.

(Nicole holds back from crying again. Nat takes Nicole's hand, removes the bandage, and examines it.)

NAT: No, no. It's not that bad, but you haven't been taking care of it. These stitches have to come out.

NICOLE: I know, we were supposed to go to the hospital two days ago. But I'm afraid . . .

NAT: Don't need the hospital. Here.

(Nat takes out his utility knife, pours vodka on it to clean it, runs it over the candle flame.)

Just look the other way for a second. *(She does)*

(Nat cuts each stitch and pulls them out.)

That'll be better now. Not that bad . . . Now, just hold on a sec, this will sting.

(He pours vodka on the wound. Nicole winces, small sob.)

Then put this on. *(He grabs the Neosporin and applies it to her wound)* In a few days it will heal up. OK?

(Nat holds her hand. Nicole weeps. Max chops wood outside.)

Hey, everything's going to be fine. You're just scared that's all.

NICOLE: I don't know what I am. I feel light-headed and weak behind my knees all the time. Is that what fear feels like?

NAT: You have to have a little faith in people.

NICOLE: Yeah. *(Beat)* Would you like some tea, Nat?

NAT: Love some.

(A stillness pervades. It is broken by Max, who enters with an armful of wood.)

MAX: Should get us through the night.

NICOLE: Nat took care of my hand.

MAX: He did?

NICOLE: It feels much better.

MAX: Oh. Thanks, Nat.

NAT: I guess I should get going.

(Nat stands. Nicole grabs his arm and stops him.)

NICOLE: No, sit down. Don't go.

MAX: Nat has to go to his meeting, Nicole.

NICOLE: I know. But after the meeting, could you come back here, Nat? *(Beat)* Could you do that, Nat? Stay here tonight. We have the room.

NAT: I dunno. I guess.

NICOLE: Thank you. That would be good.

NAT: OK. Well, then I guess I'll see you later.

(Nat goes out to his truck.)

MAX: Nicole, what are you doing? You're my wife, for God's sake!

NICOLE: "Wife"? What a strange word.

MAX: It's not strange. It's what you are.

NICOLE: Like something out of a nineteenth century novel: "He had a wife." Which means what?

MAX: It means we're partners: "For better or worse. Sickness and health." You and me.

NICOLE: I guess.

MAX: Nicole, I understand if you're frightened. But this is an extraordinary situation.

NICOLE: Yeah? Maybe this is not an extraordinary situation. Maybe this is the norm. And maybe this is the real you and the real me, you know? Here in this place. Maybe our "normal" lives, *that's* extraordinary. Artificial.

MAX: But I mean, Nat. He's been very helpful, but we don't really know him. And you've seen the way he looks at you. You're encouraging him. I just don't understand, you want him to *stay* here?

NICOLE: I feel safe when he's around.

MAX: But he's going to think he belongs here.

NICOLE: He belongs here more than we do.

MAX: So what, he's going to live with us now?

NICOLE: Sure. Like you say, it's only going to be a couple of days.

MAX: This is so fucked-up!

NICOLE: Oh, you're just realizing that?

MAX: Nicole! Don't you care about *my* feelings on this?

NICOLE: Max, I can't worry about how you "feel" right now.

MAX: Yeah, well that's the way it always is, isn't it?

NICOLE: No! It's not.

MAX: What *you* want, what *you* need. What *you* feel. You want a career—you work 24/7. You want a baby—suddenly you've got time for sex; suddenly you have time for a vacation. You feel insecure—you invite a stranger into the house. It's the Nicole show. It's always been the Nicole show. I do what *you* want to do when *you* want to do it. What I want never figures into it.

NICOLE: What you want? Gee and who's been paying the bills for the last seven years so the great artist could have time to write? So *you* could have that luxury? So *you* could hang out all day and ponder the meaning of the universe?

MAX: I write because I have to.

NICOLE: And I have to work because you have to write.

MAX: I had no idea I was such a burden!

NICOLE: No, no. I had no idea living with me was so difficult. Sorry.

MAX: So now what?

NICOLE: I look at it this way, they give you lemons, make lemonade.

MAX: I hate lemonade.

NICOLE: Well you better learn to like it Max, 'cause there's nothing else to drink.

Scene 3

Lights come up, the dawn of a dark, gloomy day. Washing hangs across the living room. We see that Nat's clothes are hung along with Max's and Nicole's.

Max, with a blanket wrapped around him, is squatting by the fire, poking at it. A bedroom door opens. Nat comes out, goes to the bathroom. Then Nat comes out of the bathroom and makes his way downstairs to the kitchen. He's wearing pieces of Max's clothing.

NAT: 'Morning.
MAX: Hmm.

(Beat.)

NAT: I'm making breakfast, you want any? Eggs, hashbrowns?
MAX: Breakfast. No, that's OK. I'm fine.

(Nat busies himself in the kitchen, peeling and slicing potatoes.)

NAT: Looks like you got that snow you wanted. More coming, either today or tonight.
MAX: Snow?
NAT: And I'll tell you. When it snows up here, it *snows*.

(Nat begins to whistle softly to himself. He's happy.)

MAX: It gets dark early up here.
NAT: Oh yeah. The nights are long this time of year.
MAX: Now I understand why prehistoric people worshipped the sun. Must be what it's like around the polar circle. There's something sad about darkness. I guess because the dark is equated with death, with emptiness, with nothingness.
NAT: You know what? You think too much.
MAX: You're part of something, something large and stable. A world. *(Laughs)* And suddenly it's eclipsed and that's frightening.
NAT: You think too much and you talk a lot.
MAX: I have to think. It's a habit of mine.

(Nat, still peeling potatoes, comes and sits with Max.)

NAT: Look, things haven't changed *that* much. In fact, things haven't changed much at all. The world's still out there. I'm still me, you're still you. We're healthy. We have a roof over our heads.

MAX: That simple, is it?

NAT: Why not?

MAX: See, back in the city, things aren't the same as up here. They're more . . . complicated. It's not enough to stay warm and get fed. There's other kinds of sustenance. Of the mind, of the soul. A life. I have a life back there. I miss it. I know it doesn't mean anything to you, but I write, my work is published. OK? People all over the country have read my work. My work is admired. I've won awards. I know this sounds ridiculous, but back in the city, I *am* somebody.

NAT: Yeah? Have you ever been on a talk show?

MAX: Once.

NAT: I'm impressed.

MAX: I'm a writer. That's all.

NAT: When I was in high school, I had a friend who was a writer. Used to tell these great stories. Funny guy.

MAX: It's not the same thing.

NAT: Why not?

MAX (*Standing*)**:** Where's Nicole? Why isn't she coming down?

NAT: I know this is going to sound like a dumb question, but if you're a writer how come I never see you do any writing?

(*Max has no answer.*)

MAX: Nicole?!

(*Nicole wanders out of the bedroom.*)

You're up early.

(*Nicole ignores Max.*)

NAT (*Returning to the kitchen*)**:** I'm making eggs, you want some?

NICOLE: Eggs? Sure. Why not?

(Nicole makes her way down. She watches Nat as he cooks.)

MAX *(To Nicole)*: Last night I dreamt I was back in the city. Of all the places to dream about, I dreamt I was in a Starbucks. Can you believe that? How trite is that? Cappuccino as metaphor.

NAT: That's funny.

MAX: So I'm drinking a latte. Eating a freshly baked raisin scone and I'm buttering it, very thinly, but perfectly with perfect fresh butter. And I have the *Times* spread out in front of me and I'm trying to decide which half of the scone to eat first, and then I hear this *beeping*. It was my beeper. I'd forgotten that I have an appointment. It's getting louder and louder.

NAT: Nicole, excuse me . . . How do you like your eggs? Scrambled, dry or soft?

NICOLE: Soft.

NAT: Hashbrowns?

NICOLE: Yum!

MAX: Never mind.

NICOLE: What, Max? We're listening. Keep going. Your beeper's getting louder, yeah.

NAT: What happened?

MAX: So uh . . . in the dream . . . I'm very late. For my appointment. And it's getting dark outside, but I haven't finished my coffee. I take a sip, I burn my tongue. I haven't eaten my scone. I haven't even read the first section of the *Times*. I *need* to read the *Times*. There's a cyclone off the coast of Calcutta I need to know about. But I'm late, so I run out into the street. And there's no streetlights. Everything's dark. And people are running and I'm running with them. We're all running in the darkness. Because we're all late. And then I realize I forgot my Palm Pilot at the Starbucks, and I turn back to get it, but I can't find the Starbucks anymore. I panic. Without my Palm Pilot, what will hap-

pen to me? You know? I was running out of time . . . and
I was . . . late.

NAT: And the moral of the story is?

MAX: No moral. It's just interesting the way I see myself in my
dreams.

NICOLE: Seems pretty accurate.

MAX: No it's not! I don't have a beeper. I hate scones. I don't
even own a Palm Pilot!

NAT: The moral of the story is always give yourself enough time.

MAX: No!

NAT: Watch out for hot coffee? You might burn your tongue?

(Nicole laughs.)

MAX: Sorry I brought it up.

NAT: The Wal-Mart got looted.

(Beat. Max goes to the fire and fusses with it, re-stacks the wood.)

The state police are starting a curfew.

NICOLE: Why?

NAT: Well, you know, this kind of situation, some people have
difficulty behaving themselves.

MAX: Running low on wood.

NAT: Hey, Max, that reminds me, good news! Slim's gonna sell
me a generator. I can hook it right up to the house and we
can have lights in here. I might even be able to get the oil
burner started.

*(Max says nothing, keeps stacking. Nat brings a plate of food
to Nicole.)*

And I was thinking, you and I might want to get up on
the roof today, take a look at the gutters, make sure everything is tight before more snow comes. And we should

put up some deer fencing. Because if we don't get more snow today, we definitely will tomorrow, definitely.

(Nicole butters some bread and brings it to Max. He doesn't touch it, he doesn't look up.)

Oh, and I almost forgot! My mom's cousin has a whole cellar full of acorn squash he's just been throwin' to his hogs. Says we can have all we can eat. How 'bout that? A little maple syrup and butter, acorn squash is good.

(Max is obsessively stacking and re-stacking the firewood.)

NICOLE: Max, please stop doing that and have something to eat.
MAX: I have to get this wood stacked.
NAT: You sure you don't want any of this? You don't know what you're missing.
NICOLE: It is good.
NAT: No brag, just fact.

(Nicole and Nat laugh. Max gets up to leave the room.)

NICOLE: Where are you going?
MAX: I have things to do.
NICOLE: What do you have to do?
MAX: I have to write.

(Max leaves.)

Scene 4

Night. Max sits alone, writing by a Coleman lamp. He is unaware of headlights that flash outside. Spoon enters from outside. She looks tired.

SPOON: Hi.

MAX: Spoon? My God.

SPOON: You look like you've seen a ghost.

MAX: It's been two weeks.

SPOON: Yeah. Well.

MAX: Are you OK?

SPOON: Sort of. Yeah.

MAX: I'm so happy to see you.

SPOON: I just came to get my stuff. I didn't think you'd be up.

MAX: I don't sleep much at the moment. I have a lot of work to do.

SPOON: It's three in the morning.

MAX: Actually, I don't sleep at all.

SPOON: You're writing?

MAX: Yes.

SPOON: You haven't heard from . . .

MAX: No . . . We thought maybe you guys found each other.

SPOON: No.

MAX: No. He's probably in Chicago by now.

(Max picks up the lantern and holds it up to Spoon. Her face is dirty.)

So . . . What happened to you?

SPOON: Nothing. Everything's fine.

MAX: Oh.

SPOON: I ran into a little trouble. But everything's OK now.

(Max notices the headlights for the first time.)

MAX: Is there someone out there?

SPOON: Yeah. A guy I met. Trucker.

MAX: Doesn't he want to come in?

SPOON: No.

MAX: Did he do this to you? *(Fingers a bruise on her cheek)*

SPOON: No. He . . . he . . .

(Spoon begins to cry.)

MAX: Oh . . .

SPOON: I got really hungry, you know? And so I found this cabin that had a freezer. And I found this frozen lasagna. And those potato puffs you just heat up in the oven. And a bottle of wine. It was so nice, it was almost normal. The only thing that was missing was a VCR. I had a little buzz from the wine and I guess I fell asleep. And then . . . there was all this bright light, through the windows . . . incredibly bright, ugly light. And there was all this pounding on the door. Like explosions. And then these men were all in the room with me. They were pulling me and grabbing at me, making me stand up. And I got angry and pushed one of them away. And someone hit me.

MAX: God.

SPOON: I woke up and they were gone. Just one guy. My friend. He'd been protecting me. Keeping them away from me. He's got a truck and he's going to give me a ride.

MAX: To where?

SPOON: North. He's going North. I'm going with him. He said he heard that the lights are on in Canada.

(Spoon heads upstairs. Max stands up.)

MAX: Your things. Your things aren't in there. I put them . . . here . . .

(Max finds Spoon's things and gets them for her.)

SPOON: Oh thanks.

MAX: You sure you're OK?

SPOON: No. Are you sure *you're* OK?

MAX: No.

SPOON: Well, at least you're writing. That's good.

MAX: Last night, I woke up and the place was so cold. Like ice. The fire had gone out. So I went out to collect some kindling. And I found myself standing in the middle of the field. No moon. Pitch dark. Freezing. The stars, so intense, piercing the sky. They were so much brighter because there was no other light.

SPOON: No moon last night.

MAX: No. And as I was watching the sky, must have been for fifteen minutes, I realized I hadn't seen one jet go over. Not one. So I waited. Freezing. I waited to see one jet. One red light blinking. I stood there for a long time and I didn't see one. The sky was just a giant vacuum, black and still. I felt so small. So anonymous. And I thought, I want to be back home. I want to be me again. This way, I'm not me. And if anything happened, if I were to get stuck up here, no one would ever find out. I'd just disappear, my whole life would disappear—all the things I've done, my work, my dreams—and no one would ever know I had ever lived.

SPOON: Yeah.

MAX: Like people who die in a plague, who die in some enormous disaster. Who were they? Who knows their names? Where are the bodies? No one really knows. If you die anonymously, does that mean you were never alive in the first place?

SPOON: I shouldn't keep my friend waiting.

MAX: No. *(She starts to go)* Spoon. It means a lot to me that you liked my story.

SPOON: It was a wonderful story. You're a wonderful writer.

MAX: Yes. I need to write. The new work is good. The best I've ever done. I'd print out some pages for you to take, but there's no printer. Wouldn't be able to plug it in if there was. I'm writing longhand for the first time in years.

SPOON: But that's good.

MAX: Yeah. I suppose it is. You better go. We'll all get together the next time . . . well, whenever.

SPOON: Bye.

(Spoon leaves. Max goes back to writing.)

Scene 5

Max is working on a legal pad by the fire. Nat and Nicole are at the table playing Scrabble. The place is much neater.

NICOLE: Max. Come on.

NAT: Yeah, Max, I'd figure you'd be pretty good at this.

MAX: I'm working.

NAT *(Getting into the game)*: There you go! C-L-O-C-K! Double letter on the K, plus double word!

NICOLE: Plus you crossed the other word, so you get the double word there too! That's . . . *(Counting)* . . . forty-seven! Wow! *(Laughing)*

NAT: I guess I got the knack.

MAX: Hey, Nat, don't eggs come from chickens? How 'bout your buddy Zeke sends over a couple of chickens? Or slaughters one of those dairy cows? A nice thick steak would be a welcome change of pace.

NAT *(With a chuckle)*: Well, I wouldn't feel right asking him to do anything like that.

MAX: You wouldn't feel right?

NAT: Nope.

MAX: You know what Jethro? I don't give a shit what you feel right doing. You're supposed to be taking care of this place, you're supposed to be taking care of *us*. And it seems to me you're doing a pretty *shitty* job of it. There's no heat. All we have to eat are eggs. You can't even find me a newspaper. *(Zeroes in on them)* Seems like you've got things all mixed up. This is my vacation, not yours.

NICOLE *(Focusing on the Scrabble)*: If I could use that K, I'd be in business. What starts with K?

MAX *(Still on Nat)*: You work for me.

NICOLE: "Krispy Kreme"?

(Nat and Nicole laugh. Neither looks at Max.)

MAX: Gee, you and my wife are getting to be such good friends! Who knows? You hang around long enough, might get lucky, huh?

NICOLE: Max, that's enough.

MAX *(To Nat)*: Don't see too many women like her up this way, do you? A real prize. Doesn't smoke. Literate. Has all her teeth. A little skinny, maybe, but feed her enough eggs, she'll fatten up.

NAT *(Staring hard at his Scrabble tiles)*: You can shut up now.

MAX: I don't have to shut up. That's my wife. This is *my* house. Fuck you.

NAT: You're mistaken, friend. This was never your house.

MAX: Yeah? Well, just remember this, *pal*, she's quite a piece of ass, but it comes at a price. You're gonna have to rake a lot of leaves to keep her in style.

NAT *(Standing, in Max's face)*: You better stop.

MAX: You gonna hit me? Huh? Right. Go clean out a gutter.

(BAM! Nat hits Max in the face, knocking him back.)

NICOLE: Oh, Max!

(Nat stands his ground, clenches his fists. Max says nothing. Holding his face, he sulks back to his writing.)

NAT: I warned him. You heard me. You heard me warn him.

(Nat sits down and stares at the tiles. Big silence all around.)

Damn. I forgot what word I was thinking of.

(Nicole goes to Max, but not getting too close.)

NICOLE *(To Max)*: This is . . . Max . . . why do you have to make everything so . . . are you OK?

NAT: I didn't hurt him. Just gave him a little tap. *(Pointing at Max)* I warned you. You can't say I didn't warn you. But no, you just can't stop talking can you? Gotta push it. Talking off the top of your head. Even if it's about your own wife. If I hadn't smacked you, who knows what woulda come outta your mouth next? Look—I don't mind that you people are a spoiled bunch. I figure you can't help yourselves. It's the way you people are, you come from someplace far from here. And I don't expect to understand. But when you cross the line, and let me tell you, I've been patient, but when you cross that line, I just say to myself, They're like children and children have to be spanked every now and then.

(Max moves away from Nicole. He goes to the kitchen and gets a glass of water.)

I don't want to be the one to do it. But I'll tell you, *sir*, and I'll tell you straight, you are not back in the big bad city, you're not back where everyone does and says whatever the hell they feel like. You're on my turf. And when you're on *my* turf, you better behave yourself. Or you're gonna get what's coming to you. *(Beat)* Now. Behave yourself and we'll all get along fine. That's all I have to say.

MAX *(From the kitchen)*: Nat. You always have a full tank of gas. I know you know where to get it. Gimme half your tank and we'll get out of here.

NAT: You don't want to do that.

MAX: Why not?

NAT: It's just not a good idea, Max. Nothing but trouble out there. Bikers. Crazies.

MAX: Fuck the bikers. We want to leave.

NAT: But where would you go?

MAX: That's my business isn't it?

NAT: Listen. I have taken care of you guys all along. And despite what you think, I like you. So take it easy, and in a few days, maybe a week, things will probably be looking up. We'll fix your heat. We'll get some supplies in. It'll be fine. We're all gonna be fine.

MAX: We're not going to be fine. Nicole isn't fine. I'm not fine. We're leaving.

NAT: Max, why don't you sit down and calm down?

(Nat comes over to console Max. Max backs away and steps into Nat's shotgun. Max grabs it and cocks it.)

MAX: Back off.

NICOLE: Max what are you doing?

MAX: Nat's going to give us gas and we're going to leave. Right now.

NAT: Please put my shotgun down.

(Nat walks toward Max.)

Mister, that's my gun and I want you to put it down. I don't like it when people touch my stuff.

NICOLE: Max, stop it.

NAT: You don't know what you're doin'. Gimme.

(Nat steps a bit closer to Max. Max points the gun at Nat.)

MAX: This is a gun.

NAT: Uh-huh.

(Nat relents, drops his hands.)

MAX: We're leaving. Nicole, go get your stuff. We'll take his truck. He's got a full tank, I know he does.

NICOLE: No.

MAX: No?

NICOLE: No.

(Max grabs her wrist, tries to move her toward the door.)

MAX: Yes! We can get to Canada. We can.

(Nicole breaks away, almost hysterical.)

NICOLE: Max! There's nowhere to go! OK? Isn't that obvious? It's too dangerous. You told me what happened to Spoon. God! Out there, out there . . . I can't!!!

MAX: This is what you wanted!

NICOLE: No. Not anymore. Not now.

(Nicole turns away from Max. She crouches down, shaking with fear. She can't face him.)

If you're doing this for me, don't, because I can't come with you. I won't come with you.

MAX: No?

NICOLE: I'm sorry.

NAT: Max, why don't you go upstairs and lie down?

MAX: I don't want to lie down. I want . . . I want to . . . I need to . . . *(Crying)* Shit!

NICOLE: Max, what are you doing? Stop it!

MAX *(Steels himself)***:** It's just . . . it's just this can't be what we think it is. It can't. It's not possible. Nicole, look at me. I'm your *husband*. I love you. You love me. We have to go. You and me. Right now.

NAT: Like she said. Go rest. You'll feel better tomorrow.

(Max turns the gun back on Nat.)

MAX: SHUT UP. JUST SHUT UP! This has nothing to do with you!

NICOLE: I'm sorry, Max.

MAX: Stop saying you're sorry! Nicole, it's OK. We're going to get out of here and what happens happens. We just need each other, right? Nicole! Look at me!

NICOLE: I *can't*, Max. Don't make me.

(Max lets the gun droop. Nat jumps forward, pushing the gun away. It goes off. Nat grabs his inner thigh and falls to the floor.)

NAT: Ahhhh! You shot me!

NICOLE: Oh God! What did you do, Max?!

NAT: I'm bleeding! Goddamn it! Ahhhh!!!

NICOLE: You shot him, Max!

MAX: No I didn't. It went off!

NAT: Damn! I told you to leave it alone! Now look what you did. My leg . . . Jesus!

MAX: No, it's . . . uh . . . let's put something on it. Wrap it.

(Max runs over to the hanging clothes and grabs a shirt. He rushes back to Nat.)

NAT: Lotta blood.

MAX: Yeah, OK.

NICOLE: Max!

NAT: I don't feel so good.

MAX: Just a sec. There.

NAT: I feel sleepy.

MAX: No, don't go to sleep! Shit, I can't find the wound.

(Pause. Nat closes his eyes. Lies back.)

NICOLE: What's he doing? Is he breathing?

MAX: Yes. But I can't . . . the blood . . .

NICOLE: But, Max, what are we going to do?

MAX: I don't know. I don't know.

NICOLE: Is he going to die?

MAX: No!

NICOLE: He is.

MAX: Nicole. Stop.

NICOLE: He's still bleeding. Look.

MAX: I can see that. I don't know, Nicole. *(Slaps Nat)* Wake up. Wake up, Nat.

(Pause. Nothing happens. Max feels Nat's throat for a pulse.)

He's alive. I think.

(The lights flicker, then illuminate. The stereo begins to play. Water begins to flow from the taps. No one says anything. The phone begins to ring. No one moves. The answering machine clicks on.)

ANSWERING MACHINE *(Woman's voice)*: Hello, this is Ted and Sondra. *(Guy's voice)* Hi! *(Woman's voice)* We're not here right now, so leave a message. If not, have a great 24/7! *(Beep)*

BILLY'S VOICE: Nicole? Are you there? I've had you on auto-dial forever! Are you guys all right?

(Nicole grabs the phone.)

NICOLE *(Into phone)*: Billy? . . . Yeah, yeah, hey! No. Uh, we had, you know, some problems, in fact things have been very . . . what? . . . oh . . . well, that's great. That's wonderful. *(Listening)* You know what? Umm, can I call you back? No, I will. In a little while. Let me call you back, OK, Billy? Thanks, hon.

(Nicole gently puts the phone back in its cradle.)

Billy says the blackout's over.

(The lights get brighter. No one moves. The lights become overwhelmingly bright. Then blackout.)

END OF PLAY

RED ANGEL

Red Angel was inspired by the film *The Blue Angel*, which starred newcomer Marlene Dietrich and the great German actor Emil Jannings. What I love about the film is its focus on female power and the arrogance of one pompous man. There have been a number of plays about men and women caught in a sexual power struggle, but somehow the men always come out on top. I wanted to do it a different way.

—E.B.

Production History

Red Angel received its first reading at Lincoln Center Theater (André Bishop, Artistic Director; Bernard Gersten, Executive Producer) in New York City, on October 18, 1999. Daniel Sullivan was the director, and Michael Gross (David), Carrie Preston (Leena) and Ryan Dunn (Phil) made up the cast. It received a second reading there, with Eric Bogosian (David), Lynn Collins (Leena), Sarah Hudnut (Agnes) and Johnathan McClain (Phil) making up the cast. It then received a reading at Manhattan Theatre Club (Lynne Meadow, Artistic Director; Barry Grove, Executive Producer) on April 24, 2002. Jo Bonney was the director, with Richard Dreyfuss (David), Hilary Swank (Leena) and Sarah Hudnut (Agnes) making up the cast. It also received a reading at Atlantic Theater Company (Neil Pepe, Artistic Director; Beth Emelson, Producing Director) in New York City, on June 23, 2003. Neil Pepe was the director, with Brent Spiner playing David and Catherine Kellner playing Leena.

In July 2002 *Red Angel* received a workshop production at Williamstown Theatre Festival (Michael Ritchie, Producer; Deborah Fehr, General Manager) in Williamstown, Massachusetts. Neil Pepe was the director, and Eric Bogosian (David), Dagmara Dominczyk (Leena), Sarah Hudnut (Agnes) and Nathan Corddry (Phil) made up the cast.

Characters

DAVID BLAU   A writing professor, late forties

LEENA, AGNES, PHIL   Graduate students, mid-twenties

Setting

David Blau's cottage on campus. The Present.

ACT ONE

Evening. Lights up on the front room of a comfortable, late Victorian cottage. An overstuffed couch, leather armchair and coffee table sit before a wall of books and a leaded picture window. A fireplace. A writing desk. A mini audio system. Lamps, Oriental rugs, newspapers, stacks of books, empty wine bottles, clothes and half-filled ashtrays clutter the cozy space. A doorway leads off to other rooms. The front door opens:

DAVID *(Off)*: The dominant male . . .

> *(Through the door comes David Blau, followed by two of his graduate students: Agnes and Phil. David tosses his house keys on the desk.)*

. . . mounts and inseminates the female, thus propagating his alpha genes, improving the species, survival of the fittest, blah-blah-blah-blah-blah. Dominance is irresistible to the female, that's the way they're built.

AGNES: What females, David? Monkeys? Lions? Goats?

(David shrugs off his jacket as a third student, Leena, enters. She carefully shuts the door behind her.)

DAVID: All *females*, whatever, wherever.

AGNES: Where do you get these totally repellent and anachronistic ideas, David?

PHIL: You ever play Agnes at table tennis? She's very dominant.

(David picks up newspapers, odd bits of clothing, dumps ashtrays, etc.)

AGNES: Phil, be quiet!

DAVID: Oh, you think she's so tough, you think Agnes is "different." She's a *woman*, Phil. Do you think she'd be marrying you if you didn't have a penis?

AGNES: That is so gross! David, in an arena as intensely socialized as the psycho-sexual, evolutionary or biological mechanics predating our postindustrial selves is irrelevant. You're sexist, that's all. According to Brownmiller . . .

DAVID: Wait a minute! "Sexist"?! "Postindustrial"?! Does "postindustrial" include porno video? Does it include Viagra? This is the way it *is*, Agnes! *Women love power*. In *men*. It turns them on. That's just a biological fact. And sex is biology. What we call love is just hormones and opportunity. Romance is for the deluded.

AGNES: You don't believe any of that crap. You're one of the most sensitive men I've ever met!

DAVID: Sensitivity does not preclude honesty. Hey, enjoy your illusions while you still can. Both of you. Till death do you part. Or divorce court, whichever comes first.

AGNES: You're just teasing me, trying to get a rise out of me!

DAVID: And you love it.

AGNES: I don't love it.

(Leena is by the bookshelves, examining the library.)

DAVID: Of course you do! Teasing is about power. Power is a turn-on.

AGNES: You're describing S&M. And I'm not into S&M.

PHIL: Well, there was that one time you tied me up with my silk neckties.

AGNES: Phil!

PHIL: I'd never seen you so happy!

(David laughs. He rubs Agnes's shoulders.)

DAVID: Don't be embarrassed, Agnes! We're all human, and all human interaction is about power. It's our psychic life blood! It's what makes life worth living. I bet your buddy, as quiet as she is, is brimming with all sorts of secret fantasies. Bondage. Rubber. Spanking. Who knows? Right, Leena?

LEENA *(Turning)*: Are you talking to me?

PHIL: I dated a masochist once. She was actually a lot of fun.

DAVID: Which do you prefer, Leena? S or M? Are you a pushy "bottom" or and an easy "top"?

LEENA: I don't know. I wasn't listening.

DAVID: We're discussing the biological foundations of male-female relationships versus postindustrial S&M.

LEENA: Oh. *(Beat)* This is an amazing library.

DAVID: Not mine. Set dressing. Highly eclectic. Note the extensive Tom Clancy collection right next to the Kierkegaard.

AGNES: From your perspective, David, as a man, it all works in your favor, so it's all a joke.

DAVID: I'm not joking. Any man in the midst of a divorce does *not* joke. *(Joining Leena, handing her a book)* Check this out, a first edition *Gravity's Rainbow*.

LEENA: Oh, I've always wanted to read that.

DAVID *(Exaggerated)*: You've never read *Gravity's Rainbow*?

LEENA *(Mocking his disbelief)*: No!

DAVID *(Exiting)*: Leena! You're doing postgraduate work in English and you've never read the essential Pynchon? Unforgivable.

AGNES: Phil, why don't you defend me?

PHIL: I don't feel so hot. I think I'm sick.

LEENA: Sick?

PHIL: My stomach, I dunno.

AGNES: Well, you were stuffing yourself at the reception, it's no wonder.

PHIL: The dean's wife was watching me!

(David returns, a bottle of wine in hand, corkscrew and four glasses in the other. He mimics a fey waiter:)

DAVID: This is a particularly excellent merlot!

AGNES: Phil's sick. His stomach.

DAVID: Phil, I saw you guzzling that god-awful wine! Tasted like grape juice and gasoline.

(David pulls the cork.)

PHIL: I liked the hors d'oeuvres. The little rolled-up things weren't that bad.

LEENA *(Over her shoulder)*: They looked like mini haggis.

DAVID: Mini haggis!!! Exactly! That's what they were! Do you know what haggis is made of, Phil? *Blood!* The coagulated blood of Scottish prostitutes.

LEENA *(Over her shoulder)*: How 'bout those cat turds, deep-fried and wrapped in bacon?

(The phone rings.)

DAVID: *Yes!* The bacon-wrapped cat turds from hell! It was the smorgasbord that satan serves in the ninth circle. You ate that shit, Phil? No wonder you're sick. You should be *dead!*

(David picks up the phone on his desk.)

(On phone) Yeah? Oh, hey! How was your flight? Uh-huh. Listen, Skip, can't talk right now I'm here with some students. Where you going to be? OK, Four Seasons. Yeah, I know the number.

PHIL:	**DAVID:**
I just don't feel so good.	OK. Right. Later.

AGNES: It's all the espresso you drink. Who drinks triple espressos? You think you're Balzac.

(David hangs up and joins the others.)

PHIL: Agnes, lay off. I'm nauseous.

AGNES: If you have nothing to say, you can hang out in coffee shops all day, you will not be inspired.

DAVID: Phil, if it's serious I can drive you to the ER, get your stomach pumped.

PHIL: I don't drink that much coffee.

AGNES: He considers Starbucks his muse.

DAVID: All I know is, I'm leaving for Rome in two weeks, pal— you miss my deadline, you will have to FedEx the pages and get your grade in September.

PHIL: I just want to do one last polish.

DAVID *(To Leena)*: See how lenient I am? You should have taken me instead of that bully Finch. *(To Phil)* How does Finch get all the beautiful women?

LEENA: Maybe beautiful women don't like leniency?

DAVID: Yeah? Was Finch hard? He *was* hard wasn't he? Bad-ass. I hear he's a real bad-ass.

LEENA: He was OK. A little too full of himself.

DAVID: As you can see, I'm nothing like that. I can't believe you missed the opportunity to work with me.

PHIL *(Grimmacing)*: I'm sorry, David, I think I have to go home.

AGNES: We just got here! One night, we get to have David to ourselves!

PHIL: Agnes! I feel like I'm dying!

AGNES: OK, OK. Well, if you're dying we better get you home. Anyway, I have to get up early because David and I are meeting to go over my novella. Can we drop you, Leena?

LEENA: Hmmmm? Yeah. Sure. I should go, too. *(To David)* I have to run home and read *Gravity's Rainbow*.

DAVID: You can borrow it if you want. Or steal it. Whatever.

AGNES: Nine A.M., David? Or should we make it earlier so we have more time?

PHIL: Agnes, I feel like shit!

DAVID: Make it eight, Agnes. Bring coffee.

AGNES: Perfect. Eight. Come on, Phil.

DAVID *(To Phil)*: Feel better!

(Agnes and Phil are out the door.)

LEENA: Well, bye!

DAVID *(To Leena)*: It was a pleasure meeting you, Leena. I really enjoyed these five minutes of intimacy. I guess I'll never see you again. So—have a nice life.

LEENA: Thank you. And I'm honestly sorry I missed out on your lectures. Finch was a total sleeping pill.

DAVID: Well, in the fall, I'll be giving a talk at the library. In the city. You should come.

LEENA: I will. Seriously.

(A honk of a horn.)

DAVID: We can have lunch. Or something.

LEENA: OK. I'd like that. I'll get the date from Agnes. Well, good night.

(David watches Leena go, then turns back into the room, wanders aimlessly picking up the bottle of wine, examining it, putting it back down. Finally he picks up the phone and dials.)

DAVID: Yes. Room 1410 please. *(Beat)* Hey. Huh? Oh come on! *NO!* They are graduate students, man. Very *advanced* graduate students. No fooling around. What am I going to do, have one stay the night so we can discuss existentialism? Been there, done that. So anyway, who's gonna be at this party? Yeah. Yeah. You think we can get an offer? Uh-huh. No, No auction. I can't wait! I'm flat, I need the bread. Susan's lawyers are breathing down my neck. No, I know. I know!

(There's a knock at the door, it opens a crack. Leena slips in. David puts one finger up as in "one sec.")

Well listen, call me from the party and tell me what happens. I'll be up, I have to read some papers, stuff like that. OK. Good. Yeah, I'm here. *(Hangs up the phone)*

LEENA: Sorry. I didn't mean to interrupt.

DAVID: No, please . . . what? Is Phil OK?

LEENA: Oh, no. I . . . left something behind. It's here somewhere.

DAVID: Oh yeah, sure. I don't remember . . . what is it?

LEENA: It's a leather bag, like a little bookbag?

(David sneaks a look through the open door.)

DAVID: Are Phil and Agnes waiting . . . ?

LEENA: Phil was all green, said he was going to puke, so I got out to walk and then I realized, so I ran back. I'm really sorry.

DAVID: No, no, *please.* Uh, where do you think you left it?

LEENA: Well, I . . . thought it was with my jacket. Shit, I hope it's not at the dean's house.

(David finds the bag by the bookshelves.)

DAVID: Here we go!

LEENA: Oh, great. Thanks.

DAVID: No prob.

LEENA: OK. Well. Good night again. *(She turns to go)*

DAVID: You on a deadline for Finch?

LEENA: Oh, no. I've turned all my work in. This is just . . .

(David picks up the opened wine bottle.)

DAVID: Oh that's good. That's good. God, I opened this and every-one's abandoned me. It's a beautiful bottle of wine. Why don't you take it with you? Find some school chums to share it with?

LEENA: I don't really hang with "school chums." So . . .

DAVID: It's a shame to waste it. You know what? Have one glass with me. Or not. Whatever. Listen to me, I sound like an old lady. I should just throw it out.

LEENA: But you're really busy. I heard you say you had to read papers.

DAVID: That's just me talking to my agent. He's out in L.A. push-ing my new novel.

LEENA: Actually, do you have any food? I didn't eat at the reception.

DAVID: I do have food! I know it's hard to believe amidst all this squalor, but it's true.

LEENA *(Flustered)*: This is ridiculous. You're just being polite. Let me get out of here and stop bothering you.

DAVID: No bother! I will not let you leave my home hungry. *(Closing the door)* Now, I have chip things and I have tuna fish and I think I have smoked oysters. And *olives!* I defi-nitely have olives. Lots of olives.

LEENA: I don't really like olives. Do you have any bread? Could I have maybe a tuna fish sandwich?

DAVID: Perhaps in the freezer? *Une baguette!* Lemme check. One tuna fish sandwich and a glass of house wine! Coming right up.

LEENA: Cool!

(David goes off.)

Listen. Don't go to any trouble. OK?

DAVID *(Off)*: Are you kidding? I'm delighted you came back. I'd just end up drinking the whole bottle by myself, get all melancholy and shoot myself.

LEENA: Was this place a mansion or something?

DAVID *(Off)*: No, no. Too small. It was a guest house for an estate that was built in the 1890s. The main house burnt down during the Depression.

LEENA: You rent it?

(David enters with a bowl of tortilla chips.)

DAVID: It's part of my "deal." The English Department seduced me with it. *(Voice)* "It's very quiet, Mr. Blau. You'll be able to do a great deal of writing." Haven't written three sentences since I got here. There's a pond in the back. Come by before I leave and we'll skinny-dip.

(David exits.)

LEENA: I wanted to take your class. But I was afraid to.

(David returns with napkins, a jar of salsa.)

DAVID: What's that?

LEENA: Nothing. *(Pointing to the picture)* Is that your son?

DAVID: Niccola. Nicky, yes. Great kid. *(Pouring)* Here's your wine. *(Hands her a glass)* I'm thawing the bread. Sit down. Sit down. *(He sits)*

(Leena takes her wine and sits in the armchair.)

The light of my life. Since his mother and I separated I don't really have anyone I can call "family," so in a way, Nicky's carried me through. Incredibly mature for his age.

LEENA: How old is he?

DAVID: Nineteen. Freshman at B.U.

LEENA: That's kind of weird.

DAVID: That he's at B.U.?

LEENA: No, that, you know, you have a kid in college. I don't think of you as that old.

DAVID: Too old to be hanging out with someone your age?

LEENA: It is kind of late at night for me to be here alone.

DAVID: Why?

LEENA: I'm a student. You're a teacher.

DAVID: Well then I guess you better get going before you turn into a pumpkin.

LEENA *(Standing)*: Maybe I should.

DAVID: Except you weren't my student and I'm not really a teacher.

LEENA: True.

DAVID: You know what? Fuck the school! Sit down! *(Leena sits)* How's your wine?

LEENA: Good. Real good.

(David sits down on the couch.)

DAVID: Let me tell you something, Leena, in my four months here, this has been the first night anyone's come by to visit me on their own volition. I don't want to scare you off.

LEENA: I don't scare that easily. But, what about your girlfriend? The one they write about in the tabloids? Didn't she visit?

DAVID: Meredith is not my girlfriend.

LEENA: She was, wasn't she?

DAVID: She starred in the movie they made of my novel. That's it. We became good friends. Still are.

LEENA: Uh-huh.

DAVID: That was all gossip. Flattering-up untrue. I don't sleep with the people I work with. Bad karma.

LEENA: OK, OK.

DAVID: You don't believe me.

LEENA: I believe you. Were you still married when they made your movie?

DAVID: As a matter of fact, yes, I was.

LEENA: So after the movie was finished, did you sleep with her then?

DAVID *(Laughing)*: Who are you, Larry King?

LEENA: It's interesting.

DAVID: No it's not.

LEENA: Of course it is.

DAVID: Oh yeah? To whom?

LEENA: To some people. Your readership.

DAVID: Well then, that leaves you out, doesn't it?

LEENA: Maybe. Where do you live in the city?

DAVID: Oh, we're back to the interview.

LEENA: It's just you were saying you'd be there in the fall. I'm curious.

DAVID: When Susan, Nicky's mom, moved out to California, I got to keep the loft downtown. Bought her out. Not cheap. I guess I'll sell it evenutally.

LEENA: Oh, then you're probably not far from my place. I'm downtown, too.

DAVID: You have a place in the city?

LEENA: That's where I live.

DAVID: Oh. Well, that's nice. So you . . . ?

LEENA: . . . commute. Take the train up here.

DAVID: Every day?

LEENA: I like the train. I read. Write. All my real friends are in the city. It's my life.

DAVID: Yeah, I remember those days.

LEENA: When you had real friends?

DAVID: When I had real friends. Right. The thing about real friends though, is some get it together and some fall by the wayside and after a while, the whole colleague thing loses its charm. My best buddy spent five years writing a novel, and when it was published *finally*, the critics skinned him alive. So you know what he did? Got married, moved to Vermont, had three kids and never wrote another word.

LEENA: Was his book any good?

DAVID: It sucked out loud.

LEENA: So he made the right choice.

DAVID: You can have friends when there's nothing at stake. But this, what I do, what I've done with my life, it's not a game. Everything's at stake. No compromises.

LEENA: *You* have a family.

DAVID: *Had.* Past tense. Although I guess I'm still a pretty good father.

LEENA: I hate my father.

DAVID: Why? Did he abuse you?

LEENA: Depends on what you mean by "abuse." He's simply in love with my mother. And I hate *her* even more.

DAVID: Actually, I think whatever you do as a parent has no real effect. Best thing to do is feed 'em, throw 'em into the streets.

LEENA: I wish my father had walked out the way you did. It would have made my life much simpler.

DAVID: Oh shit, the bread! *(Exits; from off)* I didn't walk out. My wife left me.

(Leena sips her wine and ambles over to David's writing desk, flips through some notebooks, picks one up and takes it to a floor lamp, sits in a chair and reads. David enters with a sandwich.)

What's that? What's that? Hey, hey, hey, hey! You're not reading that.

LEENA: Sorry, I . . .

(David snatches the notebook away from her and sticks it into a desk drawer.)

DAVID: You may enter my inner sanctum only if you obey the rules. And rule number one is no perusal of work in progress. Sacred. Inviolate.

LEENA: A real tyrant.

DAVID: With regard to my work I am.

LEENA: And with regard to your private life?

DAVID: In my private life I am a pussycat.

LEENA: Yeah?

DAVID: Uh-huh.

LEENA: I don't believe it.

DAVID: I am. Ask anybody. I cry at the movies. I help blind people cross the street.

LEENA: You weren't a pussycat with your fans at the reception. That kid with the nose ring was mesmerized by what you had to say. And you were so rude to him.

DAVID: I just asked him if it hurt when he blew his nose.

LEENA: And what about that woman, the one with the Wonder-bra? You were very curt with her, too.

DAVID: Because she was a complete fucking idiot! Fans come in two categories, either they don't really know the work or they are complete fucking idiots. Or a combination of the two. "Oh, Mr. Blau, I'm your biggest fan." I fall for it every time. I can't resist: "You are? Which book do you like the best?" "Well, I've only read one." This is my biggest fan don't forget. "Which one?" "Uh, I can't remember the title." I'm listing my entire résumé. "No, no, no." And then of course the punchline is, she's thinking of a book by Richard fucking Price! See, they don't really care about me or my work, they just want to make believe they are literati.

LEENA: Because we live in a role-playing society.

DAVID: That's *right*! That's exactly right. And *my* role is the part of literary figure so these people can project upon me their romantic fantasies of what literature and writing is all about. And so I play my idiotic part.

LEENA: You're not playing the writer. You *are* a writer.

DAVID: By whose standards?

LEENA: By my standards. And they're very high. *(Beat)* I've read everything you've written.

DAVID: Right. Not everything.

LEENA: Everything published. I have.

DAVID: Yeah? And what's *your* favorite? . . .

LEENA: I'm not goin' there. No way.

DAVID: Hah!

LEENA: I have to make a confession. I wanted to take your course, but I was afraid I couldn't cut the mustard.

DAVID: "Cut the mustard"?

LEENA: See, you're mocking me already!

DAVID: I'm not!

LEENA: Whatever. I was intimidated.

DAVID: This place runs a tough program, you have to have chops just to get in. You must be good, so don't tell me you're intimidated. And besides, Finch is the intimidating one. He's the ball buster.

LEENA: Finch is a lecherous, insecure dick-head.

DAVID: Did he come on to you? He did, didn't he?

LEENA: I'm sure he would have if I encouraged him.

DAVID: You should have—then busted his skinny ass.

LEENA: When I heard you'd be here this semester, I thought, OK, now I can get serious. But then, I dunno, I couldn't go through with it. See, I *have* read all your books. This was a dream come true, but I didn't have the nerve. Now I'm sounding like the sycophants you make fun of.

DAVID: No you're not. I like it, keep going.

LEENA: Listen, you can throw me outta here for saying this, but the first time I read your stuff, I thought, This guy understands. He's saying it. He's not afraid. And that's what I want to be. Brave. I want to write like that.

DAVID: I'm not brave.

LEENA: In a way I didn't want to meet you because I didn't want to be disappointed. In the person, I mean, as opposed to the writer. I wanted to keep you pure. I mean, now, meeting you, I realize I was wrong to do that. But . . . does that make sense?

DAVID *(Ironic):* I guess it's flattering in its way.

LEENA: I've read some of your books twice. You're very courageous.

DAVID: No I'm not. I'm an exhibitionist.

LEENA: Well, if you expose yourself when everyone else is hiding, that's courage.

DAVID: But not necessarily good writing.

LEENA: I don't know what makes good writing. Supposedly, that's why I'm studying. But I know what I *don't* want to do. And I don't want to contribute to this conspiracy of bullshit. We don't need more sentimental, melodramatic crap laced with pseudo-insights and fucking, piss-water truisms. If you have something to say, say it, if not, shut up. But don't waste my time and I won't waste yours.

DAVID: Wow.

LEENA: You *know* what I'm saying, because it's there in your writing. Life is a big complicated knot. We can see it, we can hold it in our hands, but we can't untie it. Bad writing is writing that tries to untie the knot. Or ignores the knot altogether.

DAVID: Now I'm sorry you didn't take my course.

LEENA: Yeah, well, I am, too, now. Too bad.

DAVID *(Smiles to himself)*: Hmmm.

LEENA: I got up early today to go to the grocery store. And there was an old wino standing outside begging for money. Said he wanted to get something to eat. I figured he was just gonna buy booze, but I didn't care, I gave him a buck anyway. When I was done buying my organic grapes and my bottled water, and I was coming out of the store, there he was, chomping on some cheap vanilla wafers. He must have bought them with the money I had given him. He threw me a big smile and said, "Thanks." A package of shit cookies! Who am I, that he's thanking *me*? What was he thanking me for? For being luckier than he is? For his pain and my lack of it?

DAVID: Better he thanks you than God.

LEENA: All I need to know is that when I see these things, someone else does too. When I read your books that's how I feel. That I'm not alone in my anger. The first time I read your stuff, I was so turned on, I stayed up all night writing. You're not just a writer, David. You're a great writer. There, I said it.

DAVID: Unfortunately for me, you are a minority in your appraisal of my talent. I'm still waiting for my National Book Award. I don't even have a Guggenheim and I'll never get a Mac-Arthur.

LEENA: Why do you need those, David? You know how good you are.

DAVID: Do I?

LEENA: You have a big following and a deal at a prestigious publishing house. They made a *movie* of your novel.

DAVID: Yes, wasn't that nice of them?

LEENA: Was it exciting?

DAVID: Oh, yeah.

LEENA: Did you get to go on set?

DAVID: No. Well, for one afternoon I felt like I was part of it all. I shook hands with what's his name and got to eat lunch in the commissary with the director who couldn't wait for me to leave. Very glamorous.

LEENA: And you made a friend. Meredith.

DAVID: You are like a dog with a *bone*!

LEENA: I'm sorry. What happened between the two of you is none of my business.

DAVID: That's right. It isn't.

LEENA: I can't help myself. I have an insatiable curiosity. It gets the better of me sometimes.

DAVID: Yeah? And what if you found out that the real David Blau does not conform in any way to your notion of who I am? That indeed you *can't* identify with me because I am, in fact, not brave, but a petty and selfish shit. Not courageous, not even that angry.

LEENA: You're aware of yourself. That's all. Maybe too aware.

DAVID: But is awareness a virtue or a self-indulgent sin?

LEENA: Awareness is never a sin. *Lying* is a sin. Living a lie is a sin.

DAVID: Listen . . . I ruined a marriage. I abandoned my son when he needed me most. My last book didn't sell. That's it. That's me. Ugly. Selfish. Probably mediocre.

LEENA: You're using your irony and self-criticism as a defense. But there's no enemy here. We're all human.

DAVID: Are we?

LEENA: What you're really trying to hide from me is what a high opinion you have of yourself. You're a narcissist.

(Pause.)

DAVID: OK. So now that you've torn me open and dissected my guts, I hope your insatiable curiosity is satiated. Because I don't think I could take anymore.

LEENA: My curiosity is *never* satiated. *(Laughs)* In fact, right now it is, what's the word? Whetted.

DAVID: *Please* don't flirt me with me, Leena. You're too beautiful and I'm too old. I might get all excited and have an aneurysm right in front of you.

LEENA: *You're* the one flirting with *me*!

DAVID: Me? I don't know how to flirt. I'm totally inept with the opposite sex.

LEENA: Uh-huh. I noticed.

DAVID: I am. Or let's just say, I should be.

LEENA: Why should you be?

DAVID: So . . . anyway. I guess you need a ride to the train station or wherever you're going . . .

LEENA: You're throwing me out because I called you a narcissist.

DAVID: No! I'm throwing you out . . . I'm *not* throwing you out! It's only that I thought . . . What time is it anyway?

LEENA: Oh, I forgot, you have that meeting with Agnes in the morning, you have to go to bed.

DAVID: No, no. Forget about that. I'm just thinking, you're going to miss your train.

LEENA: There's always another train.

DAVID: OK.

(Leena takes her plate into the kitchen. David goes over to the CD player, flips it on. Sixties French jazz.)

LEENA *(Off)*: The school must be paying you a lot.

DAVID: Not enough.

LEENA *(Off)*: So why are you here, if you're already rich?

DAVID: I thought I'd get some writing done. And I'm not rich. I publish one novel every three years for which I receive a six figure advance. *Low* six figures. When you average it out, I don't make as much money as an orthodontist from New Jersey.

(Leena returns drinking a glass of water.)

LEENA: You're still rich.

DAVID: I made a bundle on the movie. Some smart investments. When the divorce finalizes, Susan will get most of it.

LEENA: Is it hard . . . breaking up?

DAVID: Oh, no! As easy as separating Siamese twins, all you need is a very sharp knife and a taste for blood.

LEENA: Did you love each other . . . when you first got together?

DAVID: Before we had Nicky, we'd stay up all night and read my pages out loud to each other. We were soulmates. Then we had a beautiful child. We had a wonderful life. *(Beat)* Tell me about *your* work.

LEENA: *My* work?

DAVID: You're here for writing. You write.

LEENA: I write.

DAVID: What do you write?

LEENA: "What do you write?" The biggest question in my universe.

DAVID: Short stories? Plays? Comic books?

LEENA *(Smiling)*: I tried a play but I got bogged down. Some poetry I won't let anyone read. Outline for a novel. Short stories. But my work isn't where I want it to be. It's too awkward. Raw.

DAVID: Raw is good. Awkward is good.

LEENA: How can you say that? You haven't read any of it.

DAVID: Hey, it's all about risk. In that fraction of a second just before you fall on your face, therein lies the truth. Nothing's wrong with awkward, Leena. We need *more* clumsiness! *(He pours himself more wine)*

LEENA *(Beat)*: David, can I ask you for a favor?

DAVID *(Effusive)*: Anything you want, my dear.

LEENA *(Off his reaction)*: How much of that wine have you drunk?

DAVID: Very little. Too little in fact.

LEENA: I was just going to say, I wish you wouldn't talk to me the way you talk to the others.

DAVID: "The others"?

LEENA: Agnes. Phil. Your students.

DAVID: You're saying I'm being pedantic?

LEENA: Well, we're not in your class now.

DAVID: You're saying I'm being an asshole.

LEENA: No, I *love* it. I love to hear it. I love the information. But the *way* you say it, I feel like you're up here and I'm down there somewhere.

DAVID: No. Well, I've only just met you, but I don't think that. That's obvious. Right?

LEENA: Is it?

DAVID: So . . . would you like me to read something of yours?

(Leena laughs.)

Wha . . . ?

LEENA: I'm sorry.

DAVID: You're laughing at me!

LEENA: I'm not. *(Laughs again)*

DAVID: You are!

LEENA: It's just you're playing this game and it's so obvious: "Read something of yours"! I mean, you're just all over the place, dancing as fast as you can! Relax!

DAVID: You're saying I'm what? Trying to make an impression? *(Leena doesn't answer)* Get over on you? Con you?

LEENA: Think you can?

DAVID (*Flustered*): No . . . Because I'm not playing any game.

LEENA: It's OK. I think it's . . . charming.

DAVID: What is "charming"?

LEENA: You. You're charming.

DAVID: I don't think anyone has ever used that term to describe me before.

LEENA: Well, you are.

DAVID: You mean I'm doing something you find attractive?

LEENA: Oh, come off it. You *know* all the women in your class think you're hot. Agnes does.

DAVID: Agnes? You discuss me with Agnes?

LEENA: Of course! She fantasizes about you. She wants to fuck your brains out. That's obvious.

DAVID (*Intrigued*): Really? *Agnes?* (*Musing*) I've noticed she watches me in a certain way.

LEENA: What way?

DAVID: You know. I'll look up and she'll be watching me. Like she's trying to send me telepathic messages with her eyes.

LEENA (*Ironic*): Really?

DAVID: C'mon. Stop it!

LEENA: Agnes isn't the only one who watches you. I've kept an eye on you, too. Walking across campus like you don't know where you are. The absentminded professor.

DAVID: Have you?

LEENA: Of course.

DAVID: Well, I've seen you, too.

LEENA: That's so not true.

DAVID: It is.

LEENA: You mean you checked me out. Another piece of student ass. Uh-huh. I get it.

DAVID: Oh, I see, it's all right when you're checking *me* out, but if I'm checking *you* out, it's somehow perverse and undermines any interest I might have in your work. Leena, I want to read your writing because I'm sure it's very good.

LEENA: Oh yeah? You don't know anything about my writing. It could be the worst crap. As far as you're concerned, it probably is.

DAVID: You can't hide who you are. You have a point of view, that's obvious.

LEENA: It's not enough. You know that.

DAVID: Shit, anyone can write. That's not the hard part. It's being able to *see* what you've written. Throw away, begin again. It takes guts to commit radical surgery. It takes attitude. You've got that.

LEENA: You think I have guts?

DAVID: You want the truth? Yes. I think you have guts and brains.

LEENA: And tits and ass.

DAVID: Hey, Leena, I'm too old for Feminism 101. You're great looking, get over it.

LEENA: Now you're flattering me.

DAVID: So what?

LEENA: Bullshitting me.

DAVID: I have not uttered one syllable of bullshit.

LEENA: You think beauty and intelligence have something to do with talent?

DAVID: Of course! All part of something larger.

LEENA: And what would that be?

DAVID: I don't know. Beauty is subjective. It's how you move through the world and how others perceive you. Call it charisma, enlightenment, spirituality, maybe.

LEENA: Now you're really blowing it out your ass.

DAVID: I'm *not*. You obviously have a fire in your belly—and that creates a kind of energy. Like Bukowski said about Lydia Vance: "You know that she was there."

LEENA: You were my age when your first book was published. You've never had the doubts I have.

DAVID: Of course I have doubts. I've always had doubts. My life is built on a bedrock of doubt.

LEENA: I could disappear from the face of the earth, as a writer I mean, tomorrow and you wouldn't give a flying fuck. So don't tell me about intelligence or Lydia what's-her-face.

DAVID: Vance. If you're asking me if I care about another writer's work the way I care about my own, you're right, I don't. So what?

LEENA: So all this "advice" and patting me on the head, what is that? It's condescending.

DAVID: I get asked for advice, I give it.

LEENA: Who asked?

DAVID: OK. OK. So why are you here? I mean, excuse me, you introduced yourself at the reception, you came over to my place, you've read everything I've written, so I can only assume . . .

LEENA: Well, you're wrong.

DAVID *(Beat)*: All right. Sorry.

LEENA *(Laughs)*: No, don't be sorry. There's nothing to be sorry about. I'm having a great time. But, I don't know how to say this—can't I admire your work without being patronized? Maybe I'm not here to learn from you?

DAVID: OK. *(Pause)* So why are you here?

LEENA: To eat a sandwich. Drink some wine. Talk.

DAVID: I can handle that. I think.

LEENA: Maybe I'm here to teach *you*?

DAVID: Wait. Hold that thought. We need more wine.

(David leaves. Phone rings. Leena is left alone. She looks out the window. She picks up her bag, puts it down again. Finds a mirror, checks herself out. We hear David in the kitchen.)

(Off) Yeah? Really? Really? That's . . . uh-huh. Wonderful. Skip, that's great! Yeah. Yeah. OK. Go ahead. *(He hangs up)*

(David enters with an uncorked bottle of wine. Animated, he pours wine as he speaks, handing one glass to Leena.)

OK, so listen to this: my agent, Skip, is at this party in L.A. and he's chatting up this manager who is quote "a huge fan of your work" (i.e., *my* work). And this manager has just signed on *two* new big fat stars. So OK, the stars' production companies will get bound galleys of my new book in their morning mail. Very good. But wait, gets better. At this *same* party is a "Suit," a studio executive, who gets wind of this and . . .

LEENA: Where is this party?

DAVID: Sheryl Crow's house in the Hollywood Hills. She has a ranch there.

LEENA: Whoa.

DAVID: Long story short, the Suit, aware of the heat that's being generated, wants to make a preemptive strike and tells Skip maybe he's going to buy the book. Not option. *Buy.* What timing! The seven sweetest words in publishing: "Soon to be a major motion picture!"

LEENA: It's going to be a movie?

DAVID: Who knows? But it will get my book out there: major media advertising, front of store promotion, twelve-city book tour. Plus cash upfront. Production bonus. It's all good. Hooray for Hollywood. *(He toasts)*

LEENA: When will the movie come out?

DAVID: I don't give a flying fuck! I DON'T WRITE MOVIES, I WRITE NOVELS!!!!

(David plops down on the couch. Leena sits next to him.)

(Almost to himself) Good. Good. Now I can relax.

LEENA: I'm happy for you.

DAVID: Not jealous?

LEENA: No. How could I be?

DAVID: You're a writer. I've never known a writer not to be jealous of another's success.

LEENA: When they made your novel into a movie you must have felt pretty successful.

DAVID: Oh sure. It's wonderful being God.

LEENA: I bet.

DAVID: There's money. Cars on call. New clothes. Everyone suddenly finds all my books that much more scintillating. Plus I'll let you in on a little secret: success is the greatest aphrodisiac.

LEENA: You had incredible willpower not to cheat on your wife.

DAVID: I never said that.

LEENA: So you had affairs?

DAVID: It's not that simple, she—look at me, I'm talking to you about my ex-wife, like you're my therapist. Listen, drink your wine.

LEENA: Please tell me.

DAVID: Susan had her own garden to tend, her writing. And the more she tended, the less she was interested in what I was doing. And what *I* was doing was who I was. Who I *am*. I *am* my work. No excuses. That's me.

LEENA: So you didn't support her writing?

DAVID: I *did*! . . . sorry, but I did. I pushed her work to everyone I knew. I read her pages, gave her advice. *Valuable* advice. But she didn't want to hear it. She had her own friends. And I had mine. And I went a little crazy. And one night, for no obvious reason, I went ballistic, screaming, yelling, punching walls. I flipped over a glass coffee table shattering it. My son hanging on my arm, trying to stop me. It was chaos. Susan took off with Nicky, I'm not even sure where to. All I remember is standing in the middle of the room, everything shattered, my feet bleeding from the broken glass, crying.

LEENA: Yeah.

DAVID: The next morning, in the midst of the most incredible hangover, I realized that I needed her and she wasn't there. So I patched it up.

LEENA: And stopped seeing Meredith?

DAVID *(Beat)*: There's no way to rationalize it. To explain it. I love my wife. I just can't be with her.

LEENA: That's sad.

DAVID: It *is* sad. For whatever reasons, I'm a man who must live in a universe in which I am the center. As a result I am essentially alone. I have returned to what I am comfortable with—isolation.

LEENA: A lone wolf.

DAVID: You could say that. But wolves travel in a pack. I am a lone, mad rooster, blinded by the sun. Solitary, ridiculous, full of manic energy. *(Crowing)* Cock-a-doodle-doo. Try it.

LEENA *(Imitating)*: Cock-a-doodle-doo.

DAVID: No, more absurd, like this: cock-a-doodle-doo!!! *(Laughs)*

LEENA: I know all about isolation.

DAVID: We are kindred spirits, eh?

LEENA: You think?

DAVID: Possibly.

LEENA: Is that why you're telling me my work is good?

DAVID: Perhaps in some way I recognize you.

LEENA: If I were a man, you wouldn't be talking to me like this.

DAVID *(Abrupt)*: Of course I would!

LEENA: No, you wouldn't.

DAVID: Doesn't the word "colleague" mean anything to you?

LEENA: You told me about your colleagues. You don't have any. *(David can't answer)* OK. You said your work is who you are. I understand that. My work is everything to me. I can't be casual about it. I have no life outside my work.

DAVID: It's hard to think of you as a hermit.

LEENA:	**DAVID:**
Is it? You just said . . .	I mean . . .

LEENA: I don't need a life outside. I've got what I need. And all I know is, that when I'm writing, everything's OK for a while. I don't know why. It goes beyond desire. It's about survival.

DAVID: I've never heard anyone put it so well.

LEENA: David, you don't have to flatter me. I'm not going to run away. I'm ecstatic to be here with you. Right now. I really needed this.

DAVID: "This"? The pleasure of my company? The dialogue?

LEENA: More than that. The whole thing. All of it.

DAVID: Which is? . . .

(A beat. Leena speaks directly, clearly, unblinking.)

LEENA: I'm not one of these spoiled suburban kids you lecture. I'm a writer and I'm a woman. And I don't do things half way. Can you handle that?

DAVID: I guess I'll have to.

LEENA: Wait a sec. Before you dive into a bottomless pool of ironic detachment, let me ask *you* something. Do you think I know everything that's going to happen before it happens? I'm taking a risk here, too. You could crush me like a grape. I mean, you invited us up here and I thought OK. This is it. Go for it. Sure he's intimidating, but why not? I would never have invited myself.

DAVID: We're just sharing a glass of wine.

LEENA: Is that what we're doing?

(Beat.)

DAVID: I guess I had you figured for someone not so incisive.

LEENA: No. You had me figured for some bimbo graduate student. You had me figured for someone you could make a pass at and if I bit, I bit. And then how does the rest of the story go? You tell me my writing is "original" or "compelling." I stay the night and then you patronize me for a few months finally ending the relationship with a letter dismissing me but letting me know that you really "value my friendship"?

DAVID: I'm about ten moves behind you on the chessboard.

LEENA: No, you're not. And we're not playing chess.

DAVID: OK. OK. So like you said, we're all big kids here.

LEENA: I'm talking too much.

DAVID: No.

LEENA *(Laughs):* You're thinking, Is this worth it?

DAVID: No. I'm not thinking that.

LEENA: I've read your books. I know you and I know you leap before you look. You're not afraid of consequences.

DAVID: Leena. Maybe you think I'm someone I'm not. I'm a very insecure man.

LEENA: Bullshit! You're a man who is secure in every way he thinks is important. It's something I want. That kind of courage.

(Phone rings.)

DAVID: I'm secure in that way because everything else about me is so fucked-up.

(Phone rings again. David finds it and picks it up.)

Skip? Oh, Nicky! Hey man. What's up?

(David listens; he steps away from Leena.)

Well, this isn't the best time to talk—but you know, your mother just freaks like that, you can't let it get to you. *(Beat)* That's crazy. I would never do that. *(Beat)* I know. I will. *(Beat)* Listen, honey, can I call you in the morning? I'm sort of hanging out with someone here. *(Beat)* Yeah. That's right. *(Beat)* I don't know. I'll give you the answer to that tomorrow. OK, kid? *(Beat)* OK. I love you. *(Hangs up)*

LEENA: That was your son.

DAVID: Uh-huh. Nicky.

LEENA: And you'll let him know tomorrow whether you got laid or not. *(Beat)* Do you tell him about all the students you sleep with?

DAVID: I don't sleep with my students.

LEENA: No?

DAVID: No.

LEENA: Isn't that what you want to do? With me?

DAVID: You were never my student.

LEENA: That's not an answer.

DAVID: Maybe.

LEENA: If you can.

DAVID (*Laughs*): That sentence can mean so many things.

LEENA: Let me tell you something, very honestly, and you can take it or leave it?

DAVID: All right.

LEENA: I would sleep with you. And I don't care where it goes from that point on. Really. This night has been a good thing for me. I like this, a lot. It feels risky. It feels like something I've never done before. Tell you the truth, I have butterflies in my belly.

DAVID: —Yeah? I also . . .

LEENA: Let me finish. And if having sex with me would in any way make you feel good, alleviate anything bad in your day, I'm very happy to be with you. And you don't have to tell me what a wonderful writer I am. You don't have to send me a letter later. You don't have to worry about my feelings. You can have me, I'm a gift. No strings attached.

DAVID: As easy as that?

LEENA: I had no choice. I had to leave my bag here. I had to get to know you.

DAVID: And I "cut the mustard." So now I can have sex with you?

LEENA: David, that was always your option.

DAVID: Really?

LEENA: All you had to do was ask.

DAVID: And what if *I* don't want to sleep with you?

LEENA: No games, David. OK?

DAVID: OK.

(Pause.)

LEENA: So why don't you come over here and touch me?

(David considers, approaches her, kisses her, then stops.)

DAVID: I think this is . . .
LEENA: Shhhhh . . .

(Leena puts a finger to his lips. Blackout.)

ACT TWO

Later. Leena, wearing David's robe, enters from the bedroom smoking a cigarette. She looks out the window. David enters from the kitchen wearing a T-shirt and slacks, no shoes, carrying cups of tea. He hands one to her. They kiss.

LEENA: I guess I should get going.

DAVID: When's the next train?

> *(David takes a drag on her cigarette, then gives it back to her. They end up on the couch together.)*

LEENA: No more trains tonight. I'll call Agnes, crash on her couch.

DAVID: Agnes? You don't want to do that, stay here. I'll wake you with a kiss and we'll stay in bed all day. Just loll around.

LEENA: I can't imagine you "lolling" around.

DAVID: Well, we can pretend we're lolling around and then eventually I *will* want you to leave because if I don't get some writing done I get very pissy and hyper. But that doesn't mean, if you go away, I won't want you to come back.

LEENA: How about I sneak out at dawn while you're sleeping? Get the first train.

DAVID: That's your option. *(Leena moves away from him)* So you're done with all your work? How'd you do with Finch?

LEENA: He loved what I wrote.

DAVID: Let *me* read it.

LEENA: No. Not yet.

DAVID: I want to read all your stuff. *(She doesn't answer)* What will you do during summer break?

LEENA: I'll write. I always write.

DAVID: You have a job in the city?

LEENA: No job.

DAVID: So how do you support yourself? Tutor?

LEENA: Tutor? No. I don't do anything. I write.

DAVID: Trust-fund baby, eh?

LEENA: You think that's what I am?

DAVID: Waitress?

LEENA: You'd like that, wouldn't you?

DAVID: You as a waitress? You mean, as some kind of pick-up fantasy?

LEENA: Yeah. You ever do that? Pick up a waitress?

DAVID: The truth?

LEENA: The truth.

DAVID: Yes. I have. When she brought me my steak and fries, she told me she "loved my work." So I went home with her. She made great coffee in the morning.

LEENA: Really?

DAVID: Hey, I didn't force her to fuck me. Probably wrote about it in her journal. *(Beat)* So if you're not rich and you're not a waitress, how do you get by?

LEENA: Odds and ends. Bits and pieces.

DAVID: Mysterious!

LEENA: That's right. You don't have to know everything about me.

DAVID: I do! I have to know every inch of you.

LEENA: Is that so?

DAVID: The more I know about you, the more I have to know.

LEENA: And what if I don't want you to know?

(David nuzzles her.)

DAVID: Don't you like me?

LEENA: I haven't decided.

DAVID: I like you.

LEENA: Do you?

DAVID: Uh-huh. I especially like the taste of your pussy.

LEENA: Hey, wait till I piss in your mouth.

DAVID: Whoa!

(They both laugh.)

You have to admit we have a nice rhythm.

LEENA: Rhythm?

DAVID: Synchronicity. We fit together very well. Unless.

LEENA: What?

DAVID: Nothing.

LEENA: Unless I'm like that with every man I sleep with?

(Now David is lost for words.)

When you were with your wife, before it got bad, how long did it stay good?

DAVID: I can't remember right now.

LEENA: What I mean is maybe synchronicity is just hormones? Nothing more than chemicals pinging off one another. Like you were saying to Agnes.

DAVID: I've been around long enough to know when something's real.

LEENA: "Real"? That's a powerful word.

DAVID: Two people fit together physically. You feel it instantly. But two people can fit together in other ways too. Tempermentally, let's say.

LEENA: You think we do that?

DAVID: I know we do. I don't have to think about it.

LEENA: Hmmmm. What if I weren't pretty or young?

DAVID: That's not a valid question. What if I weren't famous? What if I weren't, in your words, "rich"? What if I weren't me? If you weren't you? That would be another story, wouldn't it?

LEENA: Yeah, what if, what if, what if? I think it's just biology.

(Beat. David snuggles into her.)

DAVID: Ironic. To think we've been here on this campus these past three months, passing each other every day. And now, a few days before I'm leaving, we find each other.

LEENA: Why ironic?

DAVID: Well because . . . Listen, I'd say come to Rome with me but I'll be working very hard and my friends will be shuttling me around . . .

LEENA: I don't want to come to Rome.

DAVID: No?

LEENA: I've been to Rome. Too many churches.

DAVID: So you don't mind my leaving?

LEENA: Nope.

DAVID: And I'll be back in the fall.

LEENA: You'll be speaking at the library. We're going to have lunch. Remember?

DAVID: True.

(David touches the back of Leena's neck. She turns toward him, puts her arms around him.)

I love touching you.

LEENA: Yeah? You're stronger than I thought you'd be. My father was a strong man. Too strong.

DAVID: Strong? You mean he was cruel?

LEENA: He'd drink and he'd roll in drunk, wake me up in the middle of the night, drag me out of bed, sit me at the kitchen table and argue life, point by point. He was very, very intelligent. Scream in my face about injustice. I was twelve years old. If I cried he would get even angrier. Call me a baby. Said I had caused all his problems by being born. I don't know. I cried a lot.

(David lets go of her, sips his coffee.)

DAVID: Where was your mother?

LEENA: Usually upstairs, probably listening. She knew better than to get in the middle. She didn't want to deal with him when he was like that. And besides, she liked it when things were bad between us.

DAVID: Like Gant.

LEENA: "Gant"?

DAVID: You know, Thomas Wolfe. ". . . a stone, a leaf an unfound door; of a stone, a leaf a door. And of all the forgotten faces . . ."

LEENA: What are you talking about?

DAVID: *Look Homeward Angel?* Gant. The father. The great American novel?

LEENA: Oh. Sorry.

DAVID: Gant would hurl the kerosene into the flames and howl at the stars.

LEENA *(Quietly)*: My father never howled at stars.

(Leena gets up and finds a glass of water. The phone rings.)

DAVID *(Picking up phone)*: Yeah? Oh, hi. *(Beat)* No, you didn't wake me, I'm just reading. What do you want, Susan? *(Pause)*

Yes, Nicky did call about two hours ago and I have to say, I do not appreciate you putting these ideas in his head. *(Beat)* Yes, of course he's upset when you tell him I'm going to leave you penniless! *(Beat)* Susan! *Susan!* I can't send you a check, I don't have any money. *(Listening)* You can't do that. You can't. *(Beat)* Because I *own* it. It's where I live. *(Beat)* You know what, we shouldn't even be talking. *(Beat)* Call your lawyer. Call your lawyer, because that's nuts. And leave Nicky out of this, OK?

(David hangs up the phone. Paces.)

My ex. She drags my son into the middle of this whole thing. And it's all about money. Now she's saying she's taking the loft, putting a lien on my royalties. And she tries to blackmail me by making me feel guilty about how Nicky is suffering.

LEENA: Is he suffering?

DAVID: Of course he is! And it's killing me! Worse, it's killing my work. I've become paralyzed. I can't write. I can't think.

LEENA: That's crazy.

DAVID: My life has become a prison.

LEENA: If you're not writing, something's very wrong. You have to let all this shit go.

DAVID: Easy for you to say. I'd lose everything.

LEENA: "High above the shrugging waves, the suicide pilot owns the world."

(David wanders the room, and pours himself a glass of wine from the dregs of a wine bottle.)

DAVID: What's that?

LEENA: Your words. From your second novel.

DAVID: Right.

(David drinks.)

LEENA: "High above the shrugging waves, the suicide pilot owns the world. He dives and pierces the moment. He dies and lives forever."

(Leena beams at him.)

Let it go. Fuck it.

(She takes him into her arms.)

DAVID: It felt so good being inside you.

LEENA: Well, if it felt good being inside me, you should probably be inside me. You can do whatever you want with me.

DAVID: God . . .

LEENA: Take me. Fuck me.

(David kisses her. They kiss.)

DAVID: God . . . .you feel so good. Too good. I haven't felt anything like this for a long time.

(Back at the couch, he brings his face into her belly, nuzzling her desperately.)

LEENA: Look at me.

(David looks at her, deeply.)

OK.

(She laughs, pushes herself up on top of him. They're almost fucking. The phone rings.)

DAVID: Fucking Susan. I'm not answering it.

LEENA: Maybe it's not her. Maybe it's "Skip"!

(David gets up to get the phone.)

DAVID: Yeah? Hey. *(Listens)* Wait, I can't hear you. He did? How much? No! He's not bullshitting you? Bullshit. He's bullshitting you. Uh-huh. OK. So close it! Close it and send me the check by FedEx. OK, get back to the party. *Later!*

LEENA: And? . . .

DAVID: It's a lock, the studio's buying the book.

(David kisses Leena hard, but he's so full of energy he doesn't know what to do with himself. He collects some matches, bits of newspaper and the few logs lying by the fireplace and puts a fire together.)

So tomorrow we should go for a long ride in the country. Find a country inn. Take the weekend off.

LEENA: You said you had to write?

DAVID: I don't want to write. I want to celebrate. I want to forget about everything and everybody except you and me.

LEENA: I can stay up here if you want. I just have to make a call.

(David pokes at the fire.)

DAVID: To your "boyfriend"?

LEENA: No. No boyfriend.

DAVID: That's hard to believe.

LEENA: Why?

DAVID: I'd imagine you'd get hit on constantly.

LEENA: When I get "hit on," I hit back.

DAVID: Yeah, I guess you hit on me.

LEENA: Did I?

DAVID: So, do you live alone? Roommates?

LEENA: I have sort of a roommate.

DAVID: Sort of? Another student? A girl?

(David returns to Leena on the couch.)

LEENA: More like a man.

DAVID: *"Man"?*

LEENA: It's his place. I kind of house-sit for him.

DAVID: Like a friend.

LEENA: He's a friend. I think your fire's going out.

(David goes to the fire. He stirs it up.)

DAVID: Old lover?

LEENA: Something like that.

DAVID: And now?

LEENA: Now? You mean right now? This minute?

DAVID: No, I mean nowadays. You said "no boyfriend."

LEENA: He's not my boyfriend.

DAVID: But you . . .

LEENA: Sometimes . . .

(David comes back to Leena.)

DAVID: "Sometimes." He pays the rent and you sleep with him sometimes.

LEENA: That's it, in a nutshell.

DAVID: Does he give you money?

LEENA: Is that important?

(Leena gets up. She walks away from David. He follows her.)

DAVID: So, uh, not to put too fine a point on it, how long have you known your "friend"?

LEENA: Since I was nineteen. After I left home, I came to the city. Actually I took care of his kids for a while, kind of a nanny. And we got together.

DAVID: Nineteen. Wow. So who is this guy?

LEENA: No one.

DAVID: What does he do?

LEENA: He's a real estate developer.

DAVID: Jeez! Real estate developer! How old is he?

LEENA: If you're so interested in him, I'll have a dinner party and you can meet him.

DAVID: I don't want to meet him.

LEENA: You don't?

DAVID: No!

LEENA: But you're curious about him.

DAVID: Yes. I am.

LEENA: Why?

DAVID: It's obvious isn't it? What's his name?

LEENA: I'll give you his home phone number, you can call him yourself.

DAVID: I don't want to call him. I want to fight him, right now. Challenge him to a duel. Kick his ass.

LEENA *(Beat, laughs)***:** I never thought you'd be so funny!

DAVID: I'm not being funny. I'm being very serious.

LEENA: Oh, you are? Sorry.

DAVID: No, listen, I'm just saying . . .

LEENA: What?

DAVID: Nothing.

(David walks to the books. Leena lies back down on the couch.)

Tell me you're happy.

LEENA: I'm happy.

DAVID: Why?

LEENA: Because I don't know what's going to happen next.

DAVID: How can you be so wise? You're just a kid.

LEENA: I'm not wise. I'm young and smart. I know what I am.

DAVID: You are wise. Wise and beautiful. It's starting to dawn on me. You're astonishing. Like an undiscovered country.

LEENA: You don't know me.

DAVID: I know you. I think I've always known you.

(Leena goes to the stereo and flips through a handful of CDs.)

LEENA: What are these?

DAVID: My son . . . Nicky left those here. To keep me abreast of the times.

(Leena puts on a CD: Moby's "Everytime You Touch Me" plays. She closes her eyes, dancing by herself. David sits, not sure what she's up to. Leena sees David watching her. She smiles, turns up the music, pulls David to her. He resists at first, he's awkward, then despite himself, he gets into it. They embrace, then separate. David keeps gravitating toward Leena, but she keeps her distance, urging him to dance harder. Leena closes her eyes again. So does David. Leena opens her eyes, stops dancing and watches him. He looks ridiculous, of course, trying to act like a kid. The song ends abruptly. Leena's laughter breaks the mood. David snaps out of it, looking lost. As the next song begins, David walks over to the stereo and turns it off.)

What will the neighbors think?

(Leena falls into his arms and gives him a long kiss. They drop onto the couch, spent.)

When I was fourteen, my parents shipped me off to summer camp. It was in the mountains and every day was paradise. I could read on my bunk or swim in the lake, hang out with my friends. And then suddenly things weren't so simple. There was another camp across the lake, this one for girls. And once a week we would meet around a campfire, sing songs and eye each other. And there was this one girl with pale skin, raven hair, and green eyes. I was totally smitten. Thought about her every night. All day long. I couldn't eat. I was in a daze.

(David holds Leena tightly.)

Finally I got up the gumption to talk to her. We talked every day for hours. And then she confessed she was only talking to me because she had a crush on my best friend. She felt nothing for me. But I couldn't help myself, I would sit next to her every chance I got and be interrogated endlessly about the other boy, while I fantasized kissing her lips or touching her waist. It was torture. I didn't like being in love with her. Since then I've tried to be more careful.

(Beat. Silence.)

LEENA: Do you know what I love the most about your books? Why they are so brilliant?

DAVID: No.

LEENA: The bittersweet in them. The difficulties that the characters hold inside themselves, make part of themselves. They can't figure out their problems, they just absorb them, and carry them. They are people who suffer while they live. Brave people. They'd rather be destroyed than give in.

DAVID: Yes. I suppose.

LEENA: I'm that kind of person.

DAVID: But books are fiction. Those people are fiction. You can't model your life after them. All that suffering . . . in real life . . . it's just pathetic.

LEENA: What real life? I don't know what you mean by that term.

DAVID: Of course you do.

LEENA: I have no use for real life.

DAVID: Your friend with the apartment is real life.

(David gets up and stirs the fire.)

LEENA: David? . . .
DAVID: Yeah? *(Beat)* Say it. What do you want to say?

(Leena comes up behind him, puts her arms around him.)

LEENA: Don't be "careful" with me.
DAVID: No?
LEENA: "The suicide pilot owns the world."

(They kiss.)

Touch me while I fall asleep.
DAVID: Leena . . .

(David holds her in a tender embrace.)

LEENA: What?
DAVID: Something's happening to me. I feel like I'm high. Very high. Drugged.
LEENA: Mmmmmmm.
DAVID: I can't clear my head. Can't think a straight thought.
LEENA: Let's go to bed, I hear birds chirping out there somewhere.
DAVID: Are they birds?

(Leena leads David to the bedroom. She turns to face him.)

LEENA: When I saw you at the reception I thought, He's so tough.
DAVID: I'm not.
LEENA: I didn't think you were the sentimental type.
DAVID: I warned you.
LEENA: Cautious.

DAVID: I should be more cautious with you. That's what you're saying, isn't it?

LEENA: Should you?

DAVID: I can't believe it, I'm getting hard again just by looking into your eyes.

LEENA: That's nice. Come on.

DAVID: Are you some kind of witch?

LEENA: You'll see.

(Leena takes David by the hand and leads him toward the bedroom. Blackout.)

ACT THREE

Dawn. In the gray light, David enters, a blanket draped over his shoulders. He lights a cigarette and gazes out the window. He goes out the front door in his bathrobe. Moments later he returns with a newspaper, and tries to read it, squinting in the morning light. He throws down the newspaper, stubs out the cigarette and tries to stretch. He does four push-ups. He's immediately exhausted and rolls onto his back.

David spies Leena's bag and reaches for it, rifles through it and finds some of Leena's papers, her writing. He goes to his desk, switches on a desk lamp, puts on his reading glasses and begins to read, just as the phone rings. David picks up the phone.

DAVID: Yeah? Skip. Hey man. Wait a minute, isn't it like four in the morning out there? Oh. OK. Well, listen if he likes partying, that's what you've got to do. What? No, I can't fly out there. No, I can't meet with him, does he want to buy the book or not? Because I'm leaving for Rome in a few days. I'll meet him when I get back. Just tell him. OK.

OK. Go ahead, I'll talk to you.

(David hangs up. He returns to Leena's writing, engrossed.)

LEENA *(Off)*: David?

(David returns the papers to her bag. Leena appears at the bedroom door.)

Is everything all right?

DAVID: Seems Skip's making it an all-nighter with the Suit. They're going to watch the sun come up. That's the way it is out there. The young bucks all smoke crack and take steroids. The girls get implants and vomit california rolls. I just hope they remember what they're talking about.

(Leena goes to the kitchen. She returns sipping a glass of orange juice. She sits on the couch and watches him.)

LEENA: Didn't you sleep?

DAVID: I was up. I figured something out. You're coming to Rome with me.

LEENA: I can't come to Rome.

DAVID: I'll pay for everything.

LEENA: I'll get in your way.

DAVID: No you won't.

LEENA: I won't be able to write.

DAVID: So what? This is something you have to do! We have to do it. We'll cruise the Via Veneto—I know the best place for pasta y funghi. We'll get drunk on red wine and hold hands in the Borghese Gardens. I promise, you won't have to enter one church. And I know the best suite at the Hassler. Every morning you'll have breakfast in bed.

LEENA: Romantic.

DAVID: Yes!

LEENA: I can't.

DAVID: This about your friend, the real estate guy. I'm sharing you with him.

LEENA: He wouldn't even notice I was gone.

DAVID: Tell me. What is he like?

(Pause.)

LEENA: What do you want to know?

DAVID: How tall is he?

LEENA: Taller than you.

DAVID: How old is he?

LEENA: Younger. And fit. He's very fit. He boxes. *(Beat)* You don't really want me to tell you this.

DAVID: I do. Really.

LEENA: He's . . . he's very intelligent.

DAVID: Good lover?

LEENA: He's a great lover. But . . .

DAVID: Keep going.

(David lights a cigarette.)

LEENA: Oh, and his cock is much bigger than yours. Well maybe not that much longer. But thicker.

DAVID: His cock!

LEENA: That's what you want to know, right?

DAVID: Of course not!

LEENA: I think that is what you wanted to know.

DAVID: I'm sorry I asked. Although I didn't.

(Uncomfortable silence. Leena breaks out laughing.)

LEENA: Look at your face!

(David's face gets darker.)

I'm making it all up, *David*!

DAVID: You're what? *(Confused)* What?!

LEENA: Maybe.

DAVID: Well, now I want to know. Are you?

LEENA: What do you want to know?

DAVID: Don't screw with me! Were you just making all that up? Or not?

LEENA: You're so tempermental! Sentimental and tempermental.

DAVID: I don't like this.

LEENA: What?

DAVID: You're goofing on me.

LEENA *(Laughing)*: How?

DAVID: You're laughing at me. You're mocking me.

LEENA: He can dish it out but he can't take it.

DAVID: OK, OK. Just humor me for a sec. Just tell me, tell me how you *feel* about this man who is in your life. That's a simple enough question.

LEENA: It has nothing to do with you.

DAVID: IT HAS EVERYTHING TO DO WITH ME!

LEENA: Wow.

(David walks away. He stands, his back to her.)

DAVID: Yeah, "wow."

LEENA: I'm sorry.

DAVID: No. It's just I'm getting used to you.

LEENA: I'm not like your other girlfriends?

DAVID: Girlfriends?

LEENA: Would it be better if I were more submissive? Maybe listened a little more attentively? I could look up at you with big eyes while you go on about Thomas Wolfe. I could even suck your cock while you lectured me.

DAVID: What are you talking about?

LEENA: While you "share" me?

DAVID: "Share" you? Who said anything about "share you"?

LEENA: You did. Five minutes ago.

DAVID: Never mind.

(Leena approaches David, she touches his back.)

LEENA: Don't be angry. Please?

DAVID: I'm not angry. I'm irritated.

LEENA: This has been an amazing night. For me. I'm grateful. I really like you David. I don't want to piss you off.

DAVID: *Like* me?

LEENA: Yes.

DAVID *(Ironic)*: Well, gee, I "like" you, too. A whole bunch.

LEENA: That's a good thing, isn't it?

DAVID: Do you love him?

LEENA: Who?

DAVID: Now you're being evasive.

LEENA *(Laughing again, but hugging him at the same time)*: And you're being ridiculous.

DAVID: Why, because I'm in pain?

LEENA: Pain is when there's no hope, David. Don't tell me about pain, OK? *Please?* I can't stand it when men talk like that.

DAVID: Men?

(Leena walks away from David. Nothing is said for a few moments. David finds a cigarette and lights it.)

LEENA: I'm sorry I'm irritating you. There's an early train. I'll walk to the station. Leave you alone so you can do your work.

DAVID: I didn't say anything about my work. *(Stubs out his cigarette)* Why am I smoking so much? See what you do to me?

LEENA: Why don't we stop talking and go get breakfast? Unless you want to write.

DAVID: I won't be able to write anything this morning. I'm burnt out.

LEENA: You need to recharge your batteries.

DAVID: Breakfast is a great idea. We'll go to the diner.

LEENA: This diner, do they have flapjacks? Stacks?

DAVID: Yup.

LEENA: I love flapjacks.

DAVID: Good, let's go.

LEENA: Will your waitress be there?

DAVID: My waitress?

LEENA: The one you had the tryst with. The "fan."

DAVID: That wasn't up here.

LEENA: Oh, it wasn't?

DAVID: I don't have sex with every waitress I meet!

LEENA: Oh, that's good news.

(Leena reaches out and touches David's hand, caressing it.)

Hey. I really, *really* like spending this time with you.

DAVID: Good. I like being with you, too.

LEENA: Are you happy?

DAVID: I'm more than happy. You know that.

LEENA: You don't look happy.

DAVID: No?

LEENA: No.

DAVID: Leena, I . . .

LEENA: Shhhh. Let's get some breakfast.

DAVID: Yeah.

LEENA: I'm glad you're happy.

DAVID: Good.

LEENA: Good.

(They start putting on bits of clothing from the floor, from the night before. As Leena bends over, David touches her back. She stops, she waits. He embraces and holds her close to him.)

DAVID: Let me hold you.

LEENA: Ummmmmm.

(David says nothing, just holds her, his eyes closed.)

Are you all right?

DAVID: I guess.

LEENA: Don't you want to get breakfast?

DAVID: Who are you?

LEENA: That's a strange question.

DAVID: I don't think I've ever met anyone like you.

LEENA: Maybe I'm your little campfire girl?

DAVID: I don't trust you.

LEENA: "Curiouser and curiouser."

DAVID: I think you lie to me.

LEENA: When?

DAVID: You haven't read all my books.

LEENA: No.

DAVID: Most of my books?

LEENA: Three.

DAVID: You appealed to my vanity.

LEENA: It worked. Otherwise you would never have made a move.

DAVID: What else are you lying about?

LEENA: David. Breakfast?

DAVID: I thought you were in awe of me.

LEENA: I am. And I'm not. Both.

DAVID: This is a side of you I haven't seen. Objective. Pragmatic. Cold.

LEENA: I'm not cold. That's one thing I'm not.

DAVID: That's OK. I have a well-developed protective mechanism. I won't let you hurt me.

LEENA: Jesus, David! Why would I want to hurt you?

(David watches her.)

I'm just some graduate student, if you never met me you'd never have missed me. One more pretty face.

DAVID: Yes. Except that's a lie, too, isn't it? You know you're more than that.

LEENA: I think you're projecting some kind of significance that isn't there.

DAVID: No. It's there. You know it and I know it.

LEENA: Yes.

DAVID: Come to Rome with me. You have to. It's important. It's the most important thing in the world. It's something you and I are destined to do.

LEENA: David, you're being so dramatic.

(David finds a bottle of vodka, pours himself a drink.)

You're drinking vodka at six in the morning?

DAVID: I don't understand this, what's happening between us? I thought you wanted to be with me. We just had the most amazing sex I've had in twenty years. And now you're acting completely different.

LEENA: So are you.

DAVID: You're not being you.

LEENA: And how would you know what "being me" means?

DAVID: I know.

LEENA: David. I'm just leaping without looking, what are you doing?

DAVID: I'm not leaping, I'm falling.

LEENA: "Falling"? What the fuck does that mean?

DAVID: You know, I've fallen for you and . . .

LEENA: "Fallen for me"? What's that mean?

DAVID: *Fallen*, fallen, fallen! As in *fallen* . . .

LEENA: Yeah? Finish the phrase.

DAVID: . . . in love.

LEENA: *"Love"?* C'mon David, please!

DAVID: Then "becoming obsessed."

LEENA: Yeah? "Obsessed"? How cool.

DAVID: Very obsessed. By the minute, by the second.

LEENA: It's too early in the morning for that, David! I'm hungry. Pancakes are waiting. You can be obsessed over breakfast. Then after you eat you won't be so moody.

DAVID: I'm not moody.

LEENA: Whatever you're being. Weird.

DAVID: Wait, wait, there's something I don't get. Why do you stay with this guy? This real estate developer. You must love him.

LEENA: Love is biology, remember?

DAVID: No. I take that back. I was lying. Love is essential.

LEENA: Nah. Pancakes are all I need. Let's go.

(David grabs her hard, yelling:)

DAVID: TELL ME ABOUT THIS GUY, THIS GUY IN YOUR LIFE!

(Leena stiffens. David lets go of her arm. Leena picks up her coat from the floor.)

LEENA: I gotta go. Sorry. Really, really sorry.

DAVID: Tell me! Please.

LEENA: What's wrong with you? Why are you being like this? You're going nuts.

DAVID: I love you.

LEENA: Jesus, David! Don't be an asshole!

DAVID: No, wait, that's stupid, that's a stupid stupid thing to say. I . . . I just don't know *(Stumbling)* . . . anyone . . . you're very beautiful. I know in your heart you are beautiful, I *know* you are.

LEENA: I bet you say that to all the girls.

DAVID: Stop. Fuck! I feel like I'm still drunk. We didn't drink that much did we? I have an incredible headache. Wait.

(David walks out of the room. The phone begins to ring. Leena stands and shrugs her coat on. David rushes in holding a glass of water. He picks up the phone, but has missed the call.)

Shit! *(Swallowing aspirin with his water, swallowing hard)*
Let's start over. I'm sorry.

LEENA: You're sorry? For saying you love me?

DAVID: For grabbing you.

LEENA: I have to get going. You're tired.

(Leena turns and moves toward the front door. She opens it.)

DAVID: WAIT A SECOND!

(Leena stops.)

You can't go.

LEENA: You know I should. Like you said, you're burnt out.

DAVID: No. I'm sorry. I . . . it's none of my business what you do
with your life. I don't care. I thought we . . . Oh fuck, walk
out the door, but I'm being crazy. Why am I being crazy?
I don't even know what I'm saying now.

LEENA: David—Look at me. Look me in the eyes and tell me we
have something genuine between us.

DAVID: Of course we do. That's obvious.

LEENA: What do we have?

(David tries to pull himself together.)

DAVID: Let's get breakfast. I'll tell you over breakfast.

LEENA: Do they have Canadian bacon? I love Canadian bacon.

(David goes to get his jacket.)

DAVID: They have Canadian bacon. They have Polish bacon. Sliced
haggis. All of it.

LEENA: Real maple syrup?

DAVID: They have a tanker truck hooked up to the kitchen.

LEENA: Bottomless cups of coffee?

DAVID: Bottomless cups of coffee.

(They are at the door, moving outside. Leena stops.)

LEENA: OK. And I accept your apology.

(David turns her to face him. He kisses her. He becomes impassioned and can't stop kissing her. Leena gets into the playfulness of it. She's laughing. They move away from the door and fall onto the couch and, fully clothed, in the midst of coats and clothing, David starts making love to Leena.)

DAVID: I want to. I have to. But I don't know . . . if I can.

(They are struggling. Kissing hard, but clearly he isn't getting it up.)

Fuck!

(David and Leena are a huddled mass of clothing on the couch.)

AGNES *(Off)*: David?

(David grabs the blanket and throws it over them.)

DAVID *(Under his breath)*: Shit! *(Shouting from under the blanket)* JUST A SECOND, Agnes!

(They hide as best they can.)

AGNES: What?
DAVID: It's OK. I, uh, over here.
AGNES *(Lightly)*: Good morning!

(Agnes steps into the house. She sees the mound on the couch. David's head is uncovered. He doesn't look at her.)

Darling are you all right? Are you sick?

DAVID: No. Yes, I am sick. We'll have to reschedule our meeting. Please go. Come back tomorrow.

AGNES: But it's been days!

(Leena giggles from under the cover. Agnes figures it out.)

David? Leena? Oh . . . right. Uh. We'll reschedule. That's what we should do. David. I. Darling.

(Agnes touches David's arm. He recoils.)

I . . . I better go.

(Agnes turns around and leaves. Everything's quiet. Then the huddle starts shaking. It's Leena laughing. David is holding his head.)

LEENA *(Laughing)*: Maybe . . .

DAVID: Insane. I'm going insane!

LEENA *(Laughing)*: . . . maybe . . .

DAVID: What is she thinking. Why? . . .

LEENA *(Laughing)*: Maybe we should shut the front door!

(David stands, straightens his clothing. He ambles to the front door.)

DAVID *(Shouting out the front door, almost delirious)*: CALL MY OFFICE AND WE'LL MAKE AN APPOINTMENT!

(David slams the door. He goes to his desk and jots a note.)

Meeting. Huh. Forgot all about it. Guess I'll have to pass her now.

LEENA: "Darling"? Do all your students call you . . . ?

DAVID: I have no idea why she used that word.

LEENA: That's pretty intimate.

DAVID: Well we're good friends.

LEENA: Did you have sex with Agnes, David?

DAVID: Of course not.

LEENA: Come on, David, tell me. I'm a big girl, I can take it. You had sex with her, didn't you? You had sex with Agnes. Your student.

DAVID: That's more than you need to know.

(David sits in the armchair.)

LEENA: Wow. You're a regular Don Juan. Waitresses. A student. I guess I should say, students. It must have been pretty good if she's still calling you "darling." Do you still fuck her? Were you going to fuck her while you discussed her novella?

DAVID: No!

LEENA: I know you're a devil. I know. So tell me.

DAVID: She helped me through a very difficult time.

LEENA *(Lightly, jokingly)*: I'm sure she did. And now she's in love with you.

DAVID: I dunno.

LEENA: You can tell me. *(Tickles him)* Come on, admit it!

DAVID: I honestly don't know. *(A little proud)* She says she is.

LEENA: But you don't love her.

DAVID: No! Of course not! *(Playfully protesting)* Leena, I'm a bastard.

LEENA: No you're not. You're just a liar.

(The phone rings.)

Saved by the bell.

(David picks it up.)

DAVID *(To phone)*: Yeah? Skip, wait a minute, slow down, what? Don't say that. Don't say that, Skip. So it's . . . ? But I said

I'd meet with him. This is . . . you know what? You really
screwed up. Fuck you!

*(David hangs up. Leena stands. She folds the blanket they were
hiding under.)*

Deal's off.

LEENA: What happened?

DAVID: I'm supposed to tap-dance for these people. Jump through
hoops. FUCK! I wanted . . . we were going to Rome and
I couldn't . . . FUCK!

(David picks up his coffee cup and throws it.)

LEENA: It's OK. It'll be OK. It's just a movie deal.

(David sits, he looks away.)

DAVID: What is really hard to take is that after all the work, all
the sweat, all the whatever, the value of the thing hinges
on the escapades of two suntanned fuckwits in La-La
Land. It's absurd. My work is absurd. My life is absurd.

LEENA: It doesn't alter what the book is.

DAVID: How do you know? Have you ever had a book published?
Have you?

LEENA: David . . .

DAVID: Have you?

LEENA: No.

DAVID: Then shut the fuck up!

*(David's anger is awesome. Leena is frightened. Pause. Leena,
almost in a daze, continues folding the blanket.)*

LEENA: OK.

(Pause. David goes to the couch and lies on it.)

DAVID: Listen. Come here.

LEENA: Why?

DAVID: Because I need you to. That's all.

(Leena stands over him holding the blanket.)

LEENA: You "need" me?

DAVID: Yes. I need you to stop screwing around and take care of me.

(David pulls her down to him. He kisses her hard and the blanket drops down on top of him.)

Finish what we were doing before.

LEENA: Let me see.

(Leena reaches under the blanket and strokes him.)

How does that feel?

(She gets behind him and strokes him.)

DAVID: Just keep doing that and stop torturing me.

(A moment goes by.)

LEENA: Imagine you're young. Twelve years old. Your body is beautiful. It is lithe and relaxed and full of energy. Your skin is like silk. Your penis has never been inside a woman. You are a virgin.

DAVID: Yes.

(David relaxes as Leena continues to massage him.)

LEENA: You've never seen a naked woman before. She has full breasts and hard pink nipples. Her pubic hair is moist. She is smiling and gentle and she is touching you. All over, like this. She loves you very much.

DAVID: Yes.

LEENA: She loves her little boy very much.

DAVID: Mmmmmm.

LEENA: She will take care of him, she will bring him deep inside of her. And he can do whatever he wants.

DAVID: Ohhhh..

LEENA: He can suckle. He can pee. He can do whatever he wants with her. He can come inside her body.

DAVID: Yeah.

LEENA: She's fondling his little balls and his prick. His little pink prick. She's rubbing it like this.

DAVID: Shit.

LEENA: And now she's on top. And she's pulling you inside of her. Deep inside. Her womb is hot and throbbing. She's absorbing you. She's making everything all right. She's fixing the world. You're safe.

(Leena strokes harder and harder.)

DAVID: Oh God. I can't believe this. Yes!

LEENA: Does it feel good, David? How good does this feel?

DAVID: It . . . Oh. Oh . . . It feels so good.

(David makes a little jerking motion with his body. When he stops, Leena gets off the couch. Her expression is cold.)

God.

LEENA: Did that make you happy?

DAVID: Yes.

LEENA: It's so easy to make some people happy.

(David opens his eyes. He realizes that she's no longer near him.)

DAVID: Where are you going?

LEENA: That's it, David. That's all. Now we're done.

DAVID: Done?

LEENA: Sun's up. Time to go. Lone rooster. Cock-a-doodle-doo.

DAVID: You're leaving?

LEENA: I have to get back to the city. I have to write.

DAVID: What about breakfast?

LEENA: I'm not hungry anymore.

DAVID: When you say "write," you mean you're going to see him, the real estate boxer guy.

LEENA: No, when I say "write" I mean write.

DAVID: Tomorrow?

LEENA: No. I think that's it. Don't you?

DAVID: No.

LEENA: Why?

DAVID: I want you with me in Rome.

LEENA: "With" you? I don't know what you mean when you say that.

DAVID: It's obvious.

LEENA: You can't be with someone you don't know. Not really.

DAVID: Look, we'll have breakfast, we'll take the day off. This isn't a day to work.

LEENA: I'm sorry, David. I shouldn't have come. I shouldn't have left my bag. I shouldn't have stayed. I made a mistake.

DAVID: It wasn't a mistake.

LEENA: No. This is my fault. I encouraged you. And I shouldn't have. But I wanted so badly to know what you really looked like. I thought if I were closer to you, I'd be closer to your writing. But that isn't true, is it?

DAVID: Oh, I get it. Agnes told you about us and this is some kind of revenge? Is that it?

LEENA: Agnes? No. Agnes was true blue. *(Softly)* Bye.

DAVID: What do you want me to do? I'll do it. I'm sorry. I don't want you to go. That's all. You can't go. You . . . Wait a second, *wait!* Ummm. We don't have to have sex. Again.

Ever. But I want to remain friends. Maybe I can help you with your work? I can help you set it up. Read it. It's good.

LEENA: You're lying. I can see it in your eyes.

DAVID: I'm not.

LEENA: You don't owe me anything.

DAVID: But I want to.

LEENA: Tell you what? I'll think about it and I'll call you next week.

DAVID: Next week? Promise you'll call?

LEENA: No.

(Leena heads for the door.)

DAVID: I did read your stuff. *(Beat)* It's very—

LEENA: No. I don't care.

DAVID: But I think it's very—

LEENA: I DON'T WANT TO HEAR IT!

(Beat.)

DAVID: Look at you, a frightened little girl! You are so afraid. Because you know the truth. You're nothing. And you come to me and seduce me with lies because you're nothing. And I'm something. You fuck me, but you can't love me because you're so full of fear. You want me. I know it, even if you won't say it. You whispered in my ear, "Take me!" You're a coward.

LEENA: I wanted you to take me, David. I really did. But you let me down. You fell short. You were too careful. I'm not the one who's a coward.

DAVID: Fuck you.

LEENA: Thanks for the sandwich. Have a nice time in Rome.

(David grabs her roughly.)

DAVID: You bitch!

LEENA: Hit me. Come on. Maybe I'll like you better.

(David thinks about it, then wilts.)

DAVID: Please don't go? Please?

(Leena walks out as the phone starts ringing. David doesn't answer it. He doesn't move at all.)

END OF PLAY

NON-PROFIT
BENEFIT

To inaugurate its new theater, the McCarter asked a number of us to write short plays which would be staged throughout the new building. *Non-Profit Benefit* takes place in the dressing room.

—E.B.

Production History

Non-Profit Benefit was performed in the fall of 2003 at McCarter Theatre Center (Emily Mann, Artistic Director; Jeffrey Woodward, Managing Director) in Princeton, New Jersey. The director was Ethan McSweeny, with Bruce Norris playing Bill and Michael Laurence playing Tom.

A dressing room of a regional theater. A table has been set up with coffee, and a tub of ice is filled with soft drinks and bottled water. There is also an assortment of cut-up carrots, red-bell pepper, celery and cheese cubes. A bouquet of flowers.

An actor, Bill, is talking on his cell phone, while picking at the food and sipping bottled water.

BILL: . . . No man, that's cool, I didn't expect you to come anyway. Nah. I'm only reading like one piece. Uh-huh. No, he's not here yet, so I haven't met him. But I think we're sharing the dressing room. S'posed to be a very nice guy. I guess he started in the theater. Uh-huh. So anyway, listen, about the other thing . . . No, I never got 'em. Two checks. For Ivanov, yes, that's what I'm saying. I mean, I know it's only eight hundred bucks, but you know I canceled that vacation to do it and everything and it would be nice to get it . . . uh-huh . . . Well, thanks . . . no, no, go, man, and don't worry about it. No one's agent is going to be here. OK . . . OK . . . Go . . . go . . . Bye.

(Bill fiddles with the food a bit more, grows bored. He takes out a page of script, scans it, then begins to read, watching himself in the mirror as he does. He has a certain gravity he didn't have on the phone.)

Wait, don't go yet. I want to ask you something. Should I call you my friend? No, no, I make that assumption, but it is only that—an assumption. Based not on what is true, but what I *wish* were true. I think of you as my friend, nay, even more than that, my lover. I dream about you. I've sacrificed my life for you. But, in fact, you have not returned my love. Yet I trust you, even as you smash my face into the dirt . . . humiliate me . . . degrade me . . .

(Another man, Tom, enters. He's very good looking. He watches Bill. Bill is so engrossed, he doesn't notice Tom.)

. . . and all these years, I've waited for you. Waited for consummation of our love. But I was alone, wasn't I? This was "unilateral," as the diplomats say. And you were happy to have me as a companion as long as it didn't cost you anything. But you were never going to give me what I needed . . . what I needed . . . to live . . .

(Bill is suddenly aware of Tom watching him.)

Oh.

TOM: No. I'm sorry. Go ahead.

BILL: You're Tom.

TOM: Yes.

BILL: I guess we're sharing the, uh . . . I'm Bill.

(They shake hands.)

TOM: I know. I've seen your work. Big fan.

BILL: No.

TOM: Yes. Last summer, in Williamstown . . .

BILL: Ivanov.

TOM: Yes! Brilliant. And that thing you did in Teddy's movie. Very funny.

BILL: You know Teddy? God, what am I saying? you starred in his biggest film. But, uh, thank you. I'm a big fan, too, I mean, of *you*. Your work.

TOM: Thanks.

BILL: Of all the people out there right now, you know, making Hollywood, uh, commercial film, your work, I mean, it's head and shoulders above . . .

TOM *(Fake swishy voice)*: Thtop it!

BILL: That's OK. You know. I know you know.

TOM: Have you worked with Lanie? She's so great . . .

BILL: Oh, she and I go way back. She directed me in, I know this is hard to believe, but *Hamlet* twenty years ago.

TOM: Hamlet? You?

BILL: Uh-huh.

TOM: Oh, I'd love to have seen that. Oh, wait, I *did* see that! You were wonderful! Wow, I forgot. Wow.

BILL: Yeah. Well. Emphemeral.

TOM: What?

BILL: The theater. The work. Here today, gone tomorrow.

TOM: True. Very true.

BILL: How do you know Lanie?

TOM: Oh, you know. We go back, too. In a different way.

BILL: Oh that's right! I think I knew that. I'm sorry. All part of the folklore. Of course. You two were uh . . .

TOM: Yes. Briefly . . . I was so young. And we . . . we remained friends ever since. Mainly on the phone, you know. Or when she comes to L.A. And then she called me about the benefit and I was going to be on the East Coast so I thought, Hey, you know, gotta help out the old non-profit theater . . .

BILL: And that's so great of you. I mean, the people are here tonight to see you . . . obviously . . .

TOM: Don't say that. You'll make me nervous.

BILL: It's true.

TOM: I guess. It's kind of fucked-up, don't you think?

BILL: Well, no. Movies are the culture. Movies are what people think about. And you're a star. Theater is . . . I don't know what theater is.

TOM: You've dedicated your life to it.

BILL: Yes. By default maybe. It isn't that I haven't tried to sell out. No, no. I love it. I do.

TOM (*Thoughtful*): Hollywood *is* selling out, isn't it? I mean, by its very nature. Half the things I do, I wouldn't do if I didn't get paid. *Over*paid.

BILL: No! I didn't mean it that way. Hollywood can be wonderful. Not all of it, but *your* work is wonderful. And you're giving it back. That's great.

TOM (*Earnest*): I'm going to do more theater. I've made it a goal of mine.

BILL: You have?

TOM: Yes.

BILL: Really?

TOM: In fact, this is such a strange coincidence running into you. After seeing your Ivanov last summer, I talked to some people in London and I'm doing it there in the spring.

BILL: Well that's great.

TOM: Yes. I guess the tickets are selling like hotcakes.

BILL: My goodness. That would make Anton proud.

TOM: Who? Oh, right. And what's nice is that I can be shooting a movie during the day while I'm there. We're working it all out.

BILL: Fantastic.

TOM: It is, isn't it? I feel stupid.

BILL: Why?

TOM: Because, you know, you've dedicated your whole life to the theater and I'm just a guy who did a TV series for a few years, had a hit show, went into the movies and now here I am doing theater. It's not fair . . . never mind.

BILL: No. No. I know what you're saying. It's true. The irony is true.

TOM: You should come to London.

BILL: I'd love to.

TOM: I mean it. You could coach me in the part.

BILL: *No! (As in: "Get out of here!")*

TOM: All expenses paid. First-class all the way. Think about it.

BILL: I . . .

(Uncomfortable pause.)

TOM: I better get dressed.

BILL: Yes. It must be about that time.

TOM: It's been great meeting you.

(Tom takes a Diet Coke and pops the can.)

BILL: Same here.

TOM: I admire your . . . idealism.

BILL: Likewise.

TOM *(Lifting his soda):* To Ivanov.

BILL *(Improvises, finds an already opened bottle of water):* To Ivanov.

TOM: Good luck tonight. Out there.

BILL: You, too.

TOM: Oh, fuck 'em. They love me whatever I do.

END OF PLAY